Dec. 2015

D0709174

CliffsNotes®

Parents' Guide to Paying for College and Repaying Student Loans

CliffsNotes®

Parents' Guide to Paying for College and Repaying Student Loans

by Reyna Gobel, M.B.A., M.J.

Houghton Mifflin Harcourt
Boston • New York

CliffsNotes® Parents' Guide to Paying for College and Repaying Student Loans

Copyright © 2016 by Houghton Mifflin Harcourt Publishing Company

All rights reserved.

Cover art by Jackie Shepherd

Library of Congress Control Number: 2015943210

ISBN: 978-0-544-57790-9 (pbk)

Printed in the United States of America

DOC 10 9 8 7 6 5 4 3 2 1

For information about permission to reproduce selections from this book, write to Permissions, Houghton Mifflin Harcourt Publishing Company, 215 Park Avenue South, New York, New York 10003.

www.hmhco.com

To my father, Ed Gobel, who taught me how to do math without a calculator and that the most important accomplishment anyone can do is volunteering in their community.

Acknowledgments

Thank you:

Peggy Engel, my mentor, for believing a book on repaying student loans needed to be written and that I was the one who should write it.

Grace Freedson, my literary agent, for sticking by me through fruition.

Greg Tubach, Katrina Kruse, Lori Glazer, and the rest of the gang at Houghton Mifflin Harcourt for giving me the honor of writing under the CliffsNotes brand. And, of course, my editors, Christina Stambaugh and Lynn Northrup, who kept my writing and timing on track when I started to go off on tangents.

My interviewees, who agreed to talk conversationally about their subject of expertise: Betty Lochner, Jason Washo, Ed Slott, Stacy Francis, Ryan Law, Martha Holler, Steve McCullough, Julie Hartline, Bob Bardwell, Jim Brooks, Craig Munier, and Dr. James Conover. Dr. Conover also deserves credit as my favorite finance professor.

My real-life interviewees, who trusted me enough to share their debt stories: Janae, Randy, Mary, Benjamin, Kimberly, Mickelle, Doug, and Erin.

All the editors who let a former and still occasional entertainment and pop culture writer near the subject of education. Caroline Howard, who welcomed me as a *Forbes* contributor.

My nieces and nephews: Abbi, Eddy, Eddie, David, and Jade. The other important children in my life: Jacob, Asher, Ora Bina, Eliyahu, Mendel, Yakov, Grace, Rae, Clare, and Louis. My mom and my brother Marcus and his wife Sharon.

My friends, who support me in everything that I do, including tolerating me talking endlessly about student loans and paying for college: Ambroise, Irene, Allegra, Arthur, Melanie, Gadalya, Fagie, Laurenn, Laura, Justine, Charlie, Stephanie, Nadia, Krista, Kati, Liz D., Liz H., Liz W., Camille, Anthony, Marla, Beverly, Mary, Dan, Lynnette, Carolina, Suzi, Justine, Simcha, Eileen, and Ariella.

Richard Culatta, for invaluable research help on student loan topics.

My first writing mentor, Jeff Inman, who was the first person who taught me how to write well.

Finally, I'd like to thank Brooklyn for being such an amazing place to live and work as a writer. When I want to leave my home to be around people while I write, there's never a shortage of writer-friendly cafés that let me work for hours while ordering one cup of coffee.

Table of Contents

SECTION II: LAST-MINUTE SAVINGS BOOSTS
For Parents of High Schoolers

SECTION III: FILLING THE GAPS
For Parents of In-College Students

SECTION IV: REPAYING FEDERAL AND PRIVATE STUDENT LOANS
For Parents of College Grads

About the Author

Reyna Gobel, M.B.A. and M.J., is a forbes.com education contributor, an author, and a professional speaker who's been quoted by *Money Magazine, Real Simple, and The Washington Post,* where Michelle Singletary chose the 1st and 2nd editions of *CliffsNotes Graduation Debt* as financial book of the month. She's also a continuing education instructor for the Borough of Manhattan Community College, a guest educator for the Institute for Financial Literacy, and an advice columnist and curriculum development specialist for iGrad, a financial literacy organization that provides video and written course materials on financial literacy and repaying student loans to over 300 colleges and universities. You can submit a question to her by emailing askreyna@igrad.com or tweet her at @reynagobel.

A Letter to the Reader

Dear reader,

I wrote this book because I get emails from parents who are worried about whether or not they'll be able to pay for their child's education. They'll tell me they're willing to cash out their 401K plans to do it, even if they're unemployed. Don't do that. I'm going to show you how to chip in what you can actually afford without sacrificing your own retirement and goals. You'll also get tips for how to get family to chip in a bit, too.

Beyond not depleting your own savings to save for your child's future, I'm also going to talk about how to not mortgage your own future by borrowing an excessive amount of parent loans or cosigning private loans for your children. And if you do decide to borrow loans, you'll know the best options to repay them.

This book is for parents of children who are not born yet all the way through children who have graduated college.

But don't think an early section on beginning saving for college won't help you if your kids are in high school or college. You may be able to pick up a few pointers for boosting your savings, choosing a new 529 plan, or budgeting better. Use the table of contents or the index to find information on the topics you're interested in. The section introduction pages will also give you tips on how parents of children of different ages can use those chapters.

I hope this book helps you make informed college financing decisions, while also helping you figure out how to encourage your children to find a career they'll love. Happy reading!

Best,
Reyna

Saving During the Early Years:
For Parents of Newborns Through Middle Schoolers

This section is labeled for parents of young children because it goes over the basics of starting to invest and save for your child's college education—from finding the money to start a savings plan to the basic details of a 529 plan college investment and other accounts. The information is primarily for parents of young children. However, these parents should also check out budgeting tips in other chapters and consider reading ahead to start to plan other stages of funding. This book has a thorough table of contents and an index, so you can skip around other sections easily to find topics important to your family. Parents just starting to save for their children's college education, even those with children who are in college, will still find this section useful.

Finding the Money to Start Saving for College

With tuition rising nationwide at rates over 6 percent annually, saving for college can seem like an impossible task, especially if you're still paying on your own student loans.

What kinds of numbers are parents looking at for future tuition? According to the College Board, a not-for-profit known for the AP and SAT tests, the national average cost to attend a 4-year public college including room, board, tuition, and fees for the 2014–2015 school year was nearly $19,000. If the total cost rose by just 3 percent annually, a family with a baby born this year could pay over $32,000 for the child's first year of college.

But don't fret. By the end of this book, you'll feel a lot better about the process of saving for your child's college education as part of your overall budget. You'll also learn about tax incentives, rebate programs, and state grants. Later on in this book, you'll get tips on how to tell the difference between posted price and the price you'll actually pay.

In this chapter, I talk about how you can find a few dollars within your budget to begin saving for your child's college education. In the next chapter, I cover college savings plans and tax-advantaged investment plans. In the third chapter, I go over other options for college savings and then conclude the section on a happy note: politely asking for (and getting) help from family.

Gathering Those First Dollars: Piggy Banking

When you're a new family, money may be tight. Finding those first dollars can be tough, but it isn't impossible. We'll start with one of my favorite options, saving your pennies.

Here's how this method works: If you pay for items with cash, put any change you've received in a jar when you get home. If your child is

2 years old or older, label the jar "College Savings" so they can watch it grow and get excited. They may even decide to contribute some of their allowance money.

In New York, where I live, I frequently pay with cash because many small businesses have rules against using a credit card to pay for items that are less than $5. I find I often rack up $5 in change weekly. A couple could easily save up to $10 a week with this method. Saving $5 a week adds up to $260 in annual savings or $2,600 over a decade. Saving $10 a week adds up to $520 annually; that's $5,200 over a decade. And that's only the beginning of your penny plan. A $5 weekly deposit earning a 5 percent rate of return could be worth another $700 after 10 years. With $10 a week saved at the same rate of return, you'd earn about $1,500 over 10 years. Plus, you could earn a state income tax deduction.

State income tax benefits (more about these later in Section I) can boost your savings if you decide to deposit your tax savings into your child's college savings account. For instance, if you're able to get a state income tax deduction equal to 5 percent of your 529 plan contribution, you could double the extra money you contributed yourself. That's over $3,000 earned over 10 years with a $10 weekly deposit into savings (and eventually a 529 plan college investment plan) and over $1,400 on a $5 weekly deposit. Not bad. (For more on 529 plans, see chapter 2.)

Terms Used for Earnings

Throughout this book, I'll refer to what you earn on the money you invest as *interest, earnings,* or *return on investment.* These terms all essentially represent the same result for you: money that is earned beyond the money that came out of your pocket. This is true whether the earnings came from a stock market investment, a savings account, or even a Roth IRA retirement account.

But what if you don't pay for anything via cash? After all, many people operate financially by debit or credit card. Piggy bank electronically with a savings account like the Keep the Change® Savings Program from Bank of America. With this program, all your transactions are rounded up to whole dollars. Then the difference between the actual price of the item and the dollar just above it is transferred from your checking account to your savings account.

For instance, if your transaction total is $4.14, $5.00 would be debited from your checking account and $0.86 would be transferred to your savings account. The one drawback to saving your pennies this way is your child doesn't see the growth. But you can show them bank statements when they're older and use play $1 bills in a jar to show how all your deposits are adding up. To heighten the excitement, you can have your son or daughter draw the occupation he or she wants to pursue and paste it to the jar.

If you don't have access to an automatic transfer program, calculate your piggy bank savings on a weekly basis and then transfer it to your savings account. To do this, look at your ATM transactions online. Round each one to the nearest dollar amount on a sheet of paper. Then add them together. Then subtract the exact amount of the transactions. Transfer this amount in a savings account. Since most of us keep a tally of what we spend in whole dollar amounts anyway, this shouldn't affect your budget in a negative way.

Note: *Annual growth* refers to how much your account grows per year. This amount could refer to interest earned on a savings account over a year's time and/or an increase in value on a stock market–based investment such as mutual funds containing stocks or bonds.

Making Small Contributions

Most people don't have $10,000 when they start saving for college. In fact, 40 percent of families are making small contributions, according to the College Savings Plans Network. But even small amounts add up, so get in the habit of putting something aside from your budget, even if it is only $5 or $10 per month.

If your budget can't handle it, don't fret. Check out the next section here on budget cleanup. There will also be more budgeting information throughout the book.

Budget Review

Spring cleaning generally means a list of bothersome chores, but the greatest part of cleaning up your budget is it normally frees up your money for fun stuff, too. After all, do you really enjoy paying too much for electricity, cable, phone, Internet, groceries, or insurance? Probably not. Home payments, whether rent or a mortgage, may be able to be trimmed, too, by refinancing or rent negotiation. These are just longer-termed goals.

Understand Your Budget Habits

Before you begin this exercise, I suggest you start by looking at your budget. Are you consciously spending? You can easily cut $5 to $30 of spending per day. Here's how:

Step 1: Track your spending for at least a week.

Write down everything you spend and then next to each purchase write "necessity," "fun," or "why did I buy that?" You may be surprised at the number of purchases that were truly frivolous. For instance, you may determine that you should reduce how often you go out to lunch with coworkers and instead aim to pack your lunch. Or you might notice that you waste money on groceries that will spoil because you often eat out instead of at home. As stated earlier in this chapter, putting aside just $5 per week adds up to $260 annually that you could save. One hundred dollars per month of savings × 12 months = $1,200 of extra money per year.

It's not uncommon for families to waste 25 percent of their grocery budget. In fact, I was a wishful grocery shopper. I'd always buy extra veggies in hopes that I'd eat them or I'd over-shop to avoid another trip back to the grocery store. I threw out a lot of groceries this way. Now I shop how I really live. I use a grocery shopping service to do my shopping for me, and I actually save money. They pick out great veggies and charge less than taking a cab back from the store. Plus, I never get grocery checkout shock because the shopping service generally charges per item instead of by the pound for produce. For instance, there's a price per tomato. I just select how many tomatoes I want, and I'll know the exact price when it's added to my online cart. Now, I probably have only $5 to $10 of grocery waste per month. Bad habit acknowledged; problem solved.

If your habit is going out to lunch regardless of what's in your fridge, use coupons or save half your meal from the restaurant for the next day. I've found some of my favorite restaurants, spas, and fitness classes locally in Gilt City emails. Before I moved to New York, I used restaurant.com coupons. With a promo code you find by Googling "restaurant.com promo codes," you can save up to 80 percent off a $25 gift certificate for a restaurant. Use these gift certificates for date nights or when you go out to lunch with coworkers.

The only catch to using a restaurant.com gift certificate is your bill would normally have to total $35 to use the $25 gift certificate. If you get a friend on board, you can alternate using gift certificates at different places and paying for lunch. You can also purchase $10 gift certificates that you can buy for as little as $2 with a $15 minimum purchase.

Note: In chapter 4, I talk about how you can get back money for your child's college savings from restaurant.com gift certificates and other online purchases via Upromise rewards.

In addition to using coupons, you can skip the appetizer or an extra coffee.

You should review your budget on a weekly, or at least monthly, basis to see if you're practicing smart spending.

Bottom line: Find out your habits and then work within them to maintain your lifestyle but in a smarter way.

Step 2: Put your school-aged children on a budget.

This is a great idea for two reasons: You'll get them ready to manage their expenses in college, and they'll be conscious of what they're asking you to spend. To start, sit down with your children and discuss all their expenses, from clothing to electronics to toys. Also, include extracurricular activities and school field trips in their budgets. If you don't know what costs they'll have for the school year for field trips and such, ask their teachers for an annual estimate. This information will help you plan your budget, too.

Let your children know what expenses are fixed. For instance, they can't say they'll give up a field trip or an academic activity so they can get another video game. Have them write down their spending for a week, notating "necessity," "fun," or "why did I buy that?" At the end of the week, set an allowance for them that works for what you mutually agree covers everything beyond extracurricular activities. Revisit costs once a month.

Review Your Cable, Internet, and Phone Charges

You should never throw out money, so why not look at what you're spending on utilities? For instance, I call my cable company every three months and ask about specials. Generally, I'll get 3 to 6 months of free movie channels. On the other hand, I also look at which movie channels I watch. Often, I only have a movie channel because I watch a show that's on for just 4 months out of the year. So if I cancel the channel for the other 8 months of the year, I save about $100.

Internet works the same way. Call up your Internet provider to ask if the Internet speed you're paying for is what you need for the way you use the Internet. For instance, watching TV shows or videos requires a different speed than playing certain interactive video games.

Finally, consider a bundled package with cable, Internet, and phone service to get the best deal. If you're in an area with multiple companies, make them compete for your business. Give one provider the quote from another service and see if it has a better deal. When I had multiple options for providers, I scored great deals on electric service and cable. With cable, I was offered at least a free month.

For your cell phone service, always ask if there's a better plan or a discount offered to your company's employees. It's not uncommon that you give up a 20 percent discount without realizing it—that's a potential $15 or more in monthly savings. I was able to get a shared program that basically includes me sharing data with myself. It was a group plan that doesn't require a group, and I saved over $10 per month. When close to contract renewal, ask about fee waivers on replacement phones. While a fee waiver doesn't bulk up your bank account every month, $50 saved every 2 years still adds up to $450 over 18 years. That's a lot of textbooks.

Compare and Conserve Electric Costs

Finally, let's talk about electricity use. There are two kinds of electricity savings: savings accrued by comparing rates and savings accrued by conserving energy. If you live in a state where you have a choice of electricity providers, call them and check rates.

Where I live, everyone pays the same company that acts as a payment company. However, you can choose from a variety of service companies that provide the electricity. I opted to pay a bit more for mine because I wanted to go with a company that used more renewable resources, but I make up for it, and then some, with energy conservation practices. I use reliable and effective space heaters instead of the electric heat offered in my building, and I have bamboo curtains that let in natural light. During the summer, I use quality fans and rarely need to turn on an air conditioner.

When I lived in Texas, I compared rates and was able to save $20 per month. That's $240 annually that could be used for college savings. Every state is different, but if companies want to and can compete for your business, let them.

For conservation, start with inexpensive options. These simple measures cost less than $50 and could save you a few dollars to a hundred dollars monthly on your electric bill:

- Install fluorescent light bulbs. A 15-watt fluorescent bulb uses a quarter of the electricity that a 60-watt incandescent light bulb does. And since they last longer, you'll recoup the difference in bulb costs through changing the bulbs less often. The electricity savings will go directly back into your budget.

- If your home has track lighting—lighting with multiple bulbs in a row—save it for special occasions. Track lighting may look nice, but it uses a lot of electricity—especially if you use incandescent (traditional) light bulbs instead of fluorescents. Turn these lights off immediately when you leave the room (good advice for lights in general).

- Buy smaller lamps that use only one bulb for daily use.

- Open your blinds during the day to let in natural light.

- Put your lighting on a timer. This is a great option for those who have a tendency to leave lights on when they go to bed, or if you have a home office that is only used during the day. You can buy a timer at any home store.

- According to the Department of Energy, 15 percent of your energy usage can be caused by energy leaks. If you are renting an apartment, check your windows and doors for light shining through and ask your landlord for window caulking and weather stripping when needed. If you own your home, you can pick up weather stripping at any home store and do the job yourself.

- Change air filters every three months. Dirty air filters cause your air conditioner and furnace to work harder. Changing an air filter will cost you less than $10. If you live in an apartment, you can call maintenance, and they'll change your air filter for free. If you live in an older home with odd-sized filters, there are numerous websites where you can order custom-sized air filters. Compare prices with at least three dealers and check with the Better Business Bureau (www.bbb.org) to make sure there are few or no customer complaints on the company you choose to order from.

- Use weather stripping to seal windows. Energy leaks are quite costly, but sealing windows costs just a few dollars.

·You can also save money on your monthly electric bill by making other simple changes such as buying blackout curtains or learning how to utilize your ceiling fan to save money in the winter and summer.

Be smart about when you use your curtains. During the winter, opening your blinds or curtains on a sunny day helps to heat your home. Closing them at night helps to keep the cold air out. In the summer, the opposite is true. Closing blinds or curtains during the day keeps excess heat out, while opening blinds or curtains at night lets cooler air in. For optimum energy-saving effect, get blackout curtains. These curtains have an energy-efficiency rating that rates the amount of heat or cool air blocked from outside and are best kept closed during both seasons for optimal efficiency.

Use ceilings fans year-round. Ceiling fans can warm or cool a room by a few degrees. In the summer, the clockwise motion of your fan blades circulates cool air. Just flip the switch on the base of the fan so the blades spin in the other direction when the weather changes. Remember to turn off the fan when you leave the room or turn off the lighting portion when you're using natural light.

Want to find even more ways to save energy? Contact your utilities provider and ask for a free energy audit. They may come out and tell you how you can save more on electricity and if you have energy leaks. To calculate energy savings by zip code, go to the Home Energy Saver™ website at http://hes.lbl.gov/consumer.

General Energy-Saving Tips

✓ To optimize energy efficiency without spending a dime, open your curtains during the day in the winter to let in natural light and heat from the sun to reduce heating bills.

✓ Don't run your ceiling fan when you are not in the room. It will add to your electric bill because you only feel the temperature difference in the room where the ceiling fan is on.

✓ When using your ceiling fan during the day, turn off the lighting portion, especially if your curtains or blinds are open to let in natural light.

✓ Set your thermostat 2 degrees higher in the summer and 2 degrees lower in the winter than you normally would to soak up the energy savings.

✓ When purchasing blackout curtains, look for the Energy R-Value.

✓ Change air filters every 3 months.

One-Time Events

To supplement piggy banking and other methods of setting aside small amounts of cash throughout the year, consider stashing away a portion of workplace bonuses or tax refunds. But notice that I said "a portion." I never recommend you use all of these funds for your child's college education. After all, you need emergency savings of your own.

So the best thing to do when you get a large check is to divide it up in a way that makes sense for you. For instance, in 2014 the average federal tax refund was over $3,000. Ten percent of that amount is $300; add that 10 percent up over 18 years and you'd save $5,400. With a 5 percent annual rate of return, you'd accumulate a total of $9,000 by the time your newborn is ready for college.

Note: If your income fluctuates, it's always a good idea to wait a year before depositing the money in a college savings account. You want to have money available if your income dips.

If you set aside 10 percent from workplace bonuses or other one-time events, imagine how much money you'd save.

Adding It Up

Just to show how fast your money could add up, I'll use a conservative estimate from all the above-mentioned strategies. I'll assume annual growth of 5 percent for 10 years.

- $3,300: $5 per week of piggy banking results in $3,300 before any state income tax deductions or credits are added.
- $4,000: 10 percent of a tax refund equals nearly $4,000. Workplace bonuses may or not happen, but you very well could get a federal tax refund.
- $1,300: Unsubscribing to a movie channel for 8 months if the show you watch is only on for 4 months annually: $100 per year.
- $3,100: $20 monthly in energy savings
- $3,100: $20 monthly in budget changes

Total: $14,800, without any other contributions or family help.

Remember, in the future you can also increase your savings when you go through a change in your child's needs, such as when diapers or daycare is no longer needed. For now, just be happy that you can save well over $10,000 without changing your family's lifestyle. Don't expect to fund every penny of your child's education. Be proud of yourself for taking steps to improve your budget and save for their education while still saving for your goals and needs.

Online Resources

- Bankrate.com has a wide range of great calculators. Check out their simple savings calculator to determine how your monthly savings add up when you make a budgeting change: www.bankrate.com/calculators/savings/simple-savings-calculator.aspx.

- Restaurant.com, Groupon, and other savings sites are great for finding restaurant, entertainment, and health and wellness coupons. You don't have to give up eating out altogether to save money.

Chapter Wrap-Up

- Ⓢ Saving your pennies can have big results, but you can also create virtual change by rounding up transactions to the nearest dollar and having the difference deposited into your savings account. Some banks will do this for you. If not, you can calculate the amount yourself and then transfer your change to your savings account.

- Ⓢ Review your budget to see if you're wasting money, such as spending too much on groceries that will spoil. When you understand your reasoning for your budget choices, you'll make decisions that make your family and your family's bank accounts happy.

- Ⓢ Have your children review their budgets, too.

- Ⓢ Compare all your utility costs and talk to providers about ways to reduce rates.

- Ⓢ Conserve energy without spending a lot of money or changing your lifestyle.

Choosing a 529 Plan

One of the most popular ways to save for college is in a 529 account. When you see 529 plans described as college savings plans, it sounds like these are just another type of savings account. However, there's much more to this plan than that. In fact, the 529 plan is generally more of an investment account than a savings account.

Just like an investment account you might open at a brokerage or the 401K you may have with your employer, traditional 529 plans offer a variety of investments—from savings accounts to bond- and stock-based mutual funds. Depending on which 529 plan you choose, you can select savings accounts and mutual funds individually or choose from prepackaged investments that can change as your children age. Packages are also arranged based on how much risk you want to take in hopes of the investment growing at a faster rate. The age-based plans start off allowing for more risk. Then they get more conservative as children age, switching toward safer investments such as savings accounts and short-term bonds.

Individual stocks are not part of 529 plan investments; nor are individual bonds. This is to ensure that parents don't take on bigger risks by investing large amounts in single companies. However, the only investment without any risk is a savings account. But if you only invest in a traditional savings account for 18 years, you won't earn much interest; therefore, you won't save much beyond what you deposit into the account.

The earnings from your investments grow in a 529 plan from savings account interest and from investment value increases, which are exempt from federal income tax and often from state income tax. Earnings generally aren't taxed when withdrawn unless the money isn't used for qualified education expenses such as tuition, fees, textbooks, and room and board. Thus, it's important to invest what you can reasonably afford to without expecting to withdraw funds.

In this chapter, I cover the basics you need to know about 529 plans—from investment choices to how to find out if your state might give you free money to save for your or your child's education. By the end of this chapter, you should be able to begin your research into choosing a plan.

Deciding Between a Prepaid Tuition Plan and a Traditional 529 Plan

When you purchase a 529 plan, the first major decision you need to make is whether or not you want a prepaid tuition plan or a traditional 529 plan. A prepaid tuition plan is a special type of 529 plan in which you are purchasing tomorrow's tuition based on today's tuition cost. For instance, if tuition and fees are $10,000 at a school this year, you could purchase tuition at that rate if you bought it today. Sounds great, if you happen to have $10,000 lying around, or if you happen to know exactly what school your child will attend 5, 10, or 15 years from now.

These initial investment and future predicting rules are a bit exaggerated, but they are common myths about prepaid plans. For prepaid plans, you don't have to know what school your child will attend or have all the money today. Prepaid plans offer payment plans on the tuition you buy. You can purchase units based on what you can afford. For example, parents who wanted to buy half a year of tuition in Washington State University's prepaid plan in 2014 could have paid $74 per month for 18 years at Washington's highest-priced state school. Then they could purchase more tuition in a few years when they can afford it. Even if they didn't purchase more credits, they'd have a guaranteed value for when they're ready to redeem their tuition credits purchased.

But what if you don't know what school your child will want to attend or be accepted to? After all, I don't think I would have picked the same college at 5 years old as I would in my teens or in my twenties.

If you don't know what school your child will attend, you can apply the tuition value to other accredited higher education institutions. For instance, if you bought a year of tuition at a state institution that ended up being worth $10,000, you could likely apply $10,000 toward tuition at another school outside of the state, too. So if the tuition and fees at the actual school attended are $20,000, your family would have to find other ways—loans, other savings, grants, scholarships, or student employment—to pay for the additional $10,000.

Why Wouldn't Someone Want to Buy into a Prepaid Plan?

The biggest reason is these plans aren't offered by all 50 states. College Savings Plans Network (CSPN, www.collegesavings.org) keeps a list of both the traditional and prepaid tuition 529 plans offered by all 50 states. It has a handy tool for comparing options available to you. You may be able to choose a prepaid plan if one of the child's parents or grandparents lives in a state offering the plans. When you're on www.collegesavings.org, go to Compare 529 Plans and then click on Compare Plans by State. Then click on all the states a parent or grandparent of your child lives in. You'll see right away if there's a box for a prepaid plan. For instance, if your state possibilities are Washington and Florida, both have prepaid options. However, Washington's plan uses the term *guaranteed*, while Florida's plan uses the term *prepaid*. There will always be some term, though, that is clearly distinguishable from a traditional 529 plan if offered.

For families in all 50 states, Private College 529 Plan (www.privatecollege529.com) offers parents a prepaid plan for over 270 private schools. Keep in mind that with this plan, if you take the money out instead of applying it to tuition credits, the actual monetary value is based on the amount you put in, plus or minus 2 percent. If you feel somewhat confident that your child may attend one of these schools, then it's a great value, given the annual rate of tuition inflation. On the other hand, if you question the likelihood of them attending private school, a traditional 529 plan may be a better fit, as over time you would more than likely gain more than 2 percent in earnings.

The second reason you might not use a prepaid plan is the fear that your child won't be able to attend a school outside of the state where the plan is located. That's false. Your child really can go anywhere. The differences between one prepaid plan and another is primarily what schools the automatic tuition is for, how tuition is credited if you don't choose a school within the plan, and what the value will be if your child doesn't attend college. You should ask questions about all these things before choosing a prepaid tuition plan.

A fun note: Pennsylvania has a plan for Ivy League schools, in case you're a Pennsylvania resident who knows with all your heart that your child will attend Harvard, Yale, Princeton, Brown, or the like.

Finally, the third reason why you may not want to choose a prepaid plan is versatility. In most cases, you can't save for room and board like you can in a traditional 529 plan. But you should ask about this, too. I know of only one state with a special room and board plan. As with other prepaid options, you do need to ask how the money will be applied if you don't choose one of the specific schools included.

Because of the versatility issue, families who like the safety factor of guaranteed tuition may also save separately in a traditional 529 plan for room and board, textbooks, and supplies.

Questions you should ask of any prepaid plan after checking www. collegesavings.org to see which plan you can use:

- How much does the plan cost per unit or credit? What will the unit buy me?
- What are the payment plan options?
- At what schools can I use the tuition units or credits?
- How much will I have to pay if my child chooses a different school?
- What happens if my child decides not to go to college at all?

Seven Myths About Prepaid Tuition Plans

Betty Lochner, chairwoman for the College Savings Plans Network, busts seven of the top myths surrounding prepaid plans.

Myth: Prepaid tuition plans are not 529 savings plans.

Fact: Prepaid tuition plans are 529 savings plans. In fact, prepaid tuition plans were offered in states before what is now known as traditional 529 college savings plans. Prepaid tuition plans have all the same federal and state tax benefits as other 529 plans.

Myth: You can only use your prepaid tuition account for tuition.

Fact: You can use your prepaid account not only for tuition, but also for room and board, books, or other qualified expenses. If your child chooses not to go to college or receives a scholarship, you can transfer your account to another family member, hold onto your account for a change of plans, save it for graduate school, or even request a refund.

Myth: You must use your prepaid tuition account in your home state.

Fact: You can use a prepaid tuition account at nearly any public or private college, university, or technical school in the country and even at some schools around the world. The value of your prepaid tuition account is determined by each program, but you can use the value in your account to pay college expenses practically anywhere. If the school you go to costs more than the value in your account, you will be responsible for paying the cost difference.

Myth: You lose money if you use your plan out of state.

Fact: When you use a prepaid plan out of state, you will receive an amount equivalent to what you would receive attending a public in-state school, as determined by each program. When used out of state, some plans offer a weighted average payout based on tuition at in-state institutions, and some even pay out at the highest-priced in-state public institution. Most of the time, out-of-state tuition is more costly than in-state tuition, so if a prepaid plan is going to be used at a school outside of your home state, the account owner will be responsible for paying the cost difference. The most important thing to remember is that whether used in state, out of state, or at a private institution, every dollar saved in your prepaid plan is one less dollar you have to pay out of your pocket or through school loans in the future.

Myth: Many prepaid plans have closed and others may not be available in the future.

Fact: While some states no longer offer a prepaid plan, many other states offer financially secure prepaid plans that have been around for decades and have proven to provide families with great returns on investments. Some states even provide guarantees that are particularly attractive to risk-adverse investors. Several have a full-faith backing by the legislature, so should the program run out of funds, the state is required by law to step in and fulfill its financial obligation to account owners.

It's important to note that, through two recessions, no state has walked away from its prepaid obligations or failed to ensure that benefits were paid, and no investor has lost principal in any prepaid program. Of the prepaid programs currently open to new investors, none has failed to meet its current and future obligations in full.

Myth: Prepaid plans are expensive.

Fact: Most plans have very low minimum monthly contribution limits and offer flexible payment options to make them affordable to families with budgets of all sizes.

Myth: Prepaid plans are hard to understand.

Fact: Just like any investment, families should do their homework before investing so they know what they are buying. Prepaid plans are no more difficult to understand than savings plans. If anything, prepaid plans and savings plans complement each other. If a family is able to coordinate their efforts, it might make sense to invest in both for a diversified college savings portfolio.

The Basics of Traditional 529 Plans

A traditional 529 plan accumulates money as you make contributions and then the money is invested in savings accounts or bond and mutual funds. How exactly the money is invested depends on what kind of investment plan you choose, such as whether it's a package of investments or selected individual investments. The individual investments won't include individual bonds or stocks, only funds. But the first step in researching and ultimately choosing which 529 plan you'd like to invest in is to go to www.collegesavings.org. Why? This website lists 529 plans from all 50 states with a few comparison facts such as state tax and other benefits offered.

Since state income tax benefits such as income tax deductions for contributions or potential matching grants are valuable, you don't want to overlook these benefits if they are only offered if you choose a plan in your state.

From the www.collegesavings.org website, choose Compare 529 Plans, then select Compare Plans by State. As an example, I pulled up Arkansas. It says there is a state tax benefit no matter whether you choose the ishares 529 Plan or the GIFT College Investing Plan. However, the GIFT College Investing Plan offers a matching grant program, in which the state matches your 529 plan contributions up to a certain point. It's similar to the way your employer might match your 401K contributions up to a certain amount. Often, the matching grants have income limits, although not all do. I wanted to investigate Arkansas's matching grants offer further, so I clicked on the "plan website" link for the GIFT College Investing Plan to learn more.

On the GIFT College Investing Plan home page, there is a link to the matching grants program. It says up to $500 is awarded annually per student! The income requirements indicate that families with household incomes of $30,000 or less qualify for $2 of matching grants for every $1 contributed. Thus, if a family contributed $250 to a 529 plan account, they'd receive a bonus contribution of $500. Families with household incomes in the $30,001 to $60,000 range get $1 in matching grants for every dollar contributed, up to $500 per student per year. Contributing $500 earns them another $500 from the program.

At this point, if I had a choice between the two Arkansas plans and my income qualified me for a matching grant, it would be hard for other benefits to outweigh this. But if I didn't qualify for a matching grant, I would call the state treasurer's office or read the taxation page to find out if I had to choose an Arkansas state plan to qualify for up to a $10,000 state income tax deduction for contributions as a married couple per child. If so, I would need to compare the two Arkansas plans to see which one I wanted to start with.

Arkansas does require that you choose an Arkansas plan to earn the state income tax deduction, so Arkansas residents would likely pick between the two plans. At this point, I would go back to the www. collegesavings.org page for Arkansas and start looking at other features of the plan, such as fees. Fees generally refer to a percentage charged on your account to manage the plan, as well as investment charges. Investment charges from buying and selling mutual funds are likely what makes a fee fluctuate within a range, so you'll want to view your plan choices and see what kind of investment choices will cause what fees to be charged.

For example, if you're choosing an age-based plan that gradually increases the percentage of your money that's in safer investments as your children age (money markets, savings accounts, short-term bonds), you'll want to know what the fee is for the plan you choose.

It's generally assumed that direct-sold plans that are sold directly by the plan itself will have lower fees than advisor-sold plans that are sold by advisors. However, this isn't always the case. Additionally, you'll want to check out things like how the plans are managed and typical returns on investment.

Finally, you'll notice the area of the page that talks about minimum initial contribution and minimum subsequent contribution. In the Arkansas example, someone opening the advisor-sold plan would need $500 to start and would have to contribute $50 per month. The direct-sold plan's deposit minimum is $25 to start and $10 monthly. If you can't afford the larger amount, the direct-sold option is really the only way to go.

Note: When state tax deductions and credits are less of an issue, you should check out Morningstar's ratings. Morningstar has been ranking 529 plans for years based on a variety of factors. You can find a lot of information on state plans. You'll also find articles on www.morningstar.com, as well as elsewhere when their annual rankings come out. You'll learn why Morningstar chose certain plans to earn bronze, silver, or gold medals.

A few moments to a few hours of research can make your whole process of selecting a 529 plan much easier and often more lucrative over the years. After all, wouldn't you feel bad if you carelessly selected a plan your friend had, only to find you missed out on a tax benefit or matching grant?

Note: You can have multiple plans. So if you're fortunate enough that you can contribute more than $10,000 annually—and that's your state limit for the tax deduction—to one child's 529 plan, you can consider opening a second 529 plan and choose among plans in all 50 states with anything above $10,000. A second plan may also be a good option if a plan's management changes and isn't earning as much as it used to earn. Before changing investments or plans, discuss options and charges with your plan or your financial advisor, whether or not you have an advisor-sold plan. You may be able to ask these questions during your annual planning meeting for your other investments.

Second note about the tax deduction: If you move to a different state, check on tax recapture rules before transferring 529 plan funds. Your child can still use the funds in any state they choose. Keep that plan and maybe start a second plan to benefit from your new state's tax deduction.

Debunking the Most Common 529 Plan Myths

Jason Washo, an Arizona-based personal financial specialist, dispels some of the typical myths about 529 plans.

Myth: Use it or lose it.

Fact: When a child chooses not to go to college and there are no other family members to utilize the funds, the parents don't lose the money.

The original contributions can be withdrawn tax-free and penalty-free. The earnings are taxed at ordinary income tax rates, and the earnings are subject to a penalty. To a certain degree, the earnings would have been taxed if held in another type of investment (some differences between capital gains rates and ordinary income tax rates could be argued). The only really painful loss of funds, in my opinion, is the 10 percent penalty on the earnings.

Example: Your account is currently worth $20,000. Of this, $10,000 was from earnings on investments such as mutual funds increasing in value or savings accounts earning interest. You'd get charged 10 percent of $10,000 if you withdrew everything, which equals $1,000. Then $10,000 would be taxed at your current income tax rate. If your tax rate is 25 percent, you'd get charged $2,500. The total cost to withdraw the money would be $3,500. If you decided to give your child the money to use at a later date if they decide to return to school when they're older, they wouldn't pay a tax penalty unless they withdraw the funds later. The tax penalty will likely be the same for them: 10 percent of any used funds and then an additional penalty at whatever their tax rate happens to be at the time. For instance, if your child's tax rate is 15 percent, they would owe $1,000 plus $1,500 to the IRS, provided the account doesn't grow further. But if it does grow further, why complain about extra cash? They'll still keep more than half of the additional account growth. As a side note, you can use the money for yourself later on for continuing education courses that qualify.

There are some exceptions to the penalty. In the event of the beneficiaries' death or disability, or if you distribute the assets not needed due to scholarships received, the penalty is waived.

Myth: My children won't qualify for scholarships or financial aid if I save money in a 529 plan.

Fact: Scholarships may have many different qualifying factors. Some will award benefits based on economic needs; others will be based on academic achievement; and others can be based on wide-ranging criteria. Having savings built up in a 529 or other type of account will likely not count against your child for scholarships. However, you can always ask the financial aid office at schools your child is considering if it weighs 529 plan savings a little more heavily than federal financial aid.

For federal financial aid, parents' assets are considered to be 5.6 percent available for college expenses. Students' assets are considered to be

20 percent available for expenses. Because a 529 is considered an asset of the parent, it is counted far less than other types of savings. From the Free Application for Federal Student Aid (FAFSA) process, the Expected Family Contribution (EFC) formula is much more favorable toward 529 assets than other types of accounts, such as Uniform Transfers to Minors Act accounts (UTMAs).(For more on UTMAs, see chapter 3.)

Myth: Only people with high incomes have 529 plans.

Fact: My experience is that most families opening 529 plans do so with a goal of saving a couple hundred dollars a month, often after opening the account with a few thousand dollars. There are exceptions in which a family may use a bonus to fund the accounts each year, or the sale of a business or rental property provides some extra funds to allow for lump sum funding of a college savings goal. You don't have to be rich to save for future expenses, but you do have to exercise self-discipline and make a commitment. Discipline is not a unique characteristic of any particular socioeconomic class.

Myth: You have to use 529 funds to attend colleges or universities in the same state as the plan.

Fact: This is a very common misconception among those just beginning to research 529 plans. This is because there are two different plans, pre-paid tuition 529 plans and college savings 529 plans. The first typically requires a parent or student to know where they will want to go to school. The latter, though, has flexibility and the student can choose any school that meets the requirements of being an eligible institution.

Myth: The parent must have a child before opening an account.

Fact: Parents who want to get a jump-start on saving can open an account with one parent as the beneficiary. Then after a child is born, the owner/parent can name the child as the beneficiary. Newlyweds who have an inpouring of gifts could make very good use of this plan and get savings started early—the sooner you start, the better.

Online Resources

- **www.collegesavings.org** (College Savings Plans Network): Compare 529 plans by features and by state.

- **www.morningstar.com:** See rankings of 529 plans.

- **www.privatecollege529.com:** Find prepaid plans for over 270 private schools.

- **graduationdebt.org:** Get links to articles and resources for learning more about 529 plans.

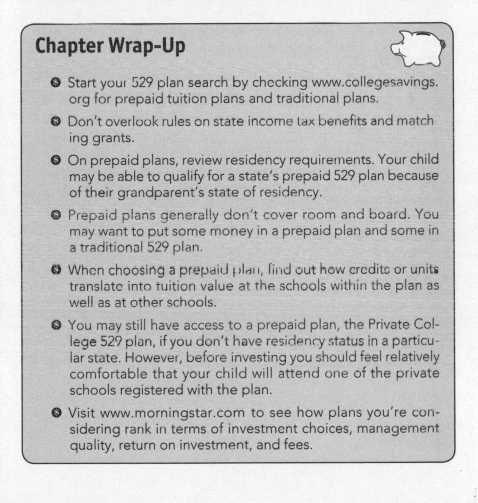

Chapter Wrap-Up

- Start your 529 plan search by checking www.collegesavings.org for prepaid tuition plans and traditional plans.

- Don't overlook rules on state income tax benefits and matching grants.

- On prepaid plans, review residency requirements. Your child may be able to qualify for a state's prepaid 529 plan because of their grandparent's state of residency.

- Prepaid plans generally don't cover room and board. You may want to put some money in a prepaid plan and some in a traditional 529 plan.

- When choosing a prepaid plan, find out how credits or units translate into tuition value at the schools within the plan as well as at other schools.

- You may still have access to a prepaid plan, the Private College 529 plan, if you don't have residency status in a particular state. However, before investing you should feel relatively comfortable that your child will attend one of the private schools registered with the plan.

- Visit www.morningstar.com to see how plans you're considering rank in terms of investment choices, management quality, return on investment, and fees.

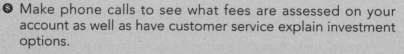 Make phone calls to see what fees are assessed on your account as well as have customer service explain investment options.

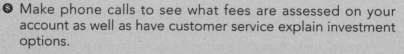 Think about if you want an aged-based plan or if you want to make individual investment choices yourself, while still understanding that the more you buy and sell investments, the more fees you could get charged.

3

Diversifying with Other Investment Options

Because of federal and often state tax benefits, 529 plans are generally the best options for saving for college. However, there are reasons why you may want to choose other or additional options.

Let's say your goal is to save enough for a private 4-year college. So you stuff as much into your 529 plan as possible. Then, 5 years down the line, you realize you've sacrificed your financial well-being and didn't save enough in your emergency account. Now, you need to take money out of your child's 529 plan.

You could pay a 10 percent penalty on the earnings portion of the withdrawal in addition to federal income tax charged on the balance.

For instance, if you took out $10,000 and $5,000 was from investment growth, you'd pay $500 on the $5,000 that was earned by investment growth. Plus, you'd pay ordinary income tax on the same $5,000. If your tax rate is 25 percent, that's another $250. This is in addition to anything the state tries to recoup from income tax breaks you received on contributions or earnings. That's why it's important that you always think of your emergency savings, too; that way you're less likely to need to take out money saved for your child's education.

Another reason you should also save outside of a 529 plan is you want to save for expenses that aren't considered qualified education expenses by the Internal Revenue Service and can't be taken out of a 529 plan without penalty, such as your future college grad visiting home during their studies.

In this chapter, I discuss saving within your own savings accounts and investment plan, saving in special savings and investment accounts under your child's name, and saving partially within a Roth IRA (an individual retirement account).

Saving Within Your Own Savings Accounts and Investments

If there's one thing I want to emphasize in this book, it's that saving for your child's future shouldn't come at the cost of your own. Thus, accumulating a significant amount of savings in your own savings accounts before deciding how much you want to save for your child is not a bad strategy.

Another strategy for making sure you save for both your and your child's future is setting aside an amount you can handle from your budget into your child's college savings account, maybe $25 per month. With this size deposit, you can manage depositing $25 into your savings, too.

Either way, when your child is ready for college, you should take a look at your investments and savings accounts and see what you can afford to give your child without hurting your long-term lifestyle. You can also just wait until you have 6 months of emergency savings and other personal savings goals accomplished before depositing additional funds into a 529 plan account.

Remember, unlike 529 plans, you will pay taxes on earnings. For instance, you will have to pay capital gains tax on investments you sell, and you will have to pay taxes on savings account interest. You also won't get the state income tax benefits you would for 529 plan benefits. However, if you saved beyond your means in a 529 plan, you could owe federal tax penalties on withdrawals for the portion of your account that was from earnings and also face potential tax recapture on state income tax benefits you received for 529 plan contributions.

However, anything you deposit into a 529 plan account that started in your investment accounts will still be eligible for state income tax benefits and federal-tax-free growth from that point on. For instance, let's say you withdrew $5,000 from your investment accounts to deposit into a 529 plan account. Your state has a 5 percent income tax and offers a tax deduction on 529 plan distributions. You'll reduce your state income tax payment or increase your refund by $250. You'll have to pay the capital gains tax on the amount of the $5,000 that was earnings, but you won't have to pay additional taxes on the growth as long as the money in the 529 plan account is used for qualified educational expenses. So if the investment grows by another $500 in the 529 plan, that amount can potentially be used for education tax-free.

Think carefully about what you can afford to save in a 529 plan account. Talk with a financial advisor at least once to discuss your overall financial picture, including college savings and investing goals.

Saving Under Your Child's Name: UTMAs

UTMAs are a wonderful alternative to 529 plans when you are open to your child using the money for something else besides education, such as starting a business or for expenses during college that aren't able to be taken out tax-free from 529 plans. You can also use these funds for your child's expenses before college.

So first off, what in the world is an UTMA? UTMA stands for Uniform Transfer to Minors Act account. It's simply a savings or investment account under your child's name. You can set up one of these accounts by checking off a box at your bank. You can also set up an investment account with your financial advisor or other brokerage that includes a variety of investments of your choosing.

Unlike 529 plans, UTMAs have tax advantages, and there is no penalty for withdrawal for noneducational expenses if you need the money for something else.

So, why would anyone choose a 529 plan if these plans offer the same tax advantage with more flexibility? There are three reasons.

Limits on tax benefits: Federal-income-tax free earnings, growth from investments and savings accounts, is capped (in 2015, it's capped at $1,050 annually). The cap may not matter early in savings for a middle-class family depositing $100 monthly, but it could as money adds up and investments increase.

For instance, let's use two examples. Both average a 5 percent growth on the account annually. For an account to earn $1,050 or more in investment growth, a $20,000 account balance is required.

After the first $1,050 in earnings, the next $1,050 is taxed; it incurs a kiddie tax, a tax paid on the child's tax return based on their earnings. Young children more than likely will not earn any income and won't be taxed. A high school student who has a year-round part-time job, however, may end up paying tax, but it will likely be at a rate much lower than the parents' rate. If the account earns more than $2,100 in a year, then parents will have to pay taxes on the remaining amount at their marginal income tax rate (the amount at which the last dollar they earn is taxed). This is likely so wealthy individuals don't stuff money into accounts under their children's names to avoid paying taxes.

You can't take money out of the account for yourself, but you can withdraw money from the account for the child's expenses, such as food, clothing, housing, and school supplies.

In addition, parents may want to take advantage of state income tax benefits for contributions to 529 plans. For instance, contributing

$10,000 when state income tax is assessed at a 5 percent rate could save families $500 per year that could be spent on something besides taxes. If $1,000 is contributed over the course of a year that would still yield $50 in tax savings.

Ownership: If you choose an UTMA over a 529 plan, the money belongs to your child on their 18th birthday. With a 529 plan, you still maintain control as the owner and can dole out funds to pay for qualified education expenses. If your child doesn't use all the money, you can change the beneficiary name to one of their siblings or yourself. You can also take the tax penalty and withdraw the remaining balance.

Age-based options: 529 plans will automatically adjust your investment mix as children age, so the investment mix gradually gets safer by leaning toward a larger percentage in money markets and savings accounts. Without this option, you would have to decide when you want to sell each mutual fund, bond fund, and so on, and also decide what and if to buy something else in its place.

Bottom line: UTMAs are a great option for saving for your child's education for expenses that don't qualify to be withdrawn federal-income-tax-free from 529 plans or if you opt to give the money to your child upon high school graduation to use for something other than education, such as seed money to start a business or a down payment on their first home.

Investing in Roth IRAs as Part of College Savings Planning

When you're deciding between investing in additional college savings or additional retirement savings, Roth IRAs maybe the answer. Why?

Roth IRAs, individual retirement accounts, are contributed after taxes, so you've already paid taxes on the income you're investing. This is no different than the way 529 plans work. Roth IRAs also grow tax-free similar to 529 plans.

But Roth IRAs have a big benefit for college savers: Withdrawing for college tuition is an excused reason for withdrawing without penalty. This benefit makes Roth IRAs a great way to hedge bets if you don't feel comfortable with how much you have saved for retirement when your child is young.

This doesn't mean Roth IRAs are better than 529 plans when you know you can afford to stock X amount of money in a 529 plan. By saving with a Roth IRA alone, you could miss out on state grants or tax benefits on contributions to a 529 plan or tax deductions on the federal or state level that you might have received on contributions for other types of retirement accounts. You could also miss out on matching funds from your employer on your 401K if you're not fully funding up to the match limit.

As with all types of college savings and investment choices, remember these are all options and can be combined as best fits your family's needs.

Debunking Common Roth IRA Myths

CPA, retirement expert, founder of www.irahelp.com, and creator of the Public Television show *Ed Slott's Retirement Roadmap*, Ed Slott debunks common Roth IRA myths.

Myth: You're limited in investment choices.

Fact: The main investment options that are excluded from Roth IRAs (and traditional IRAs) are collectibles and life insurance. You have more choices than in a 401k or 529 plan because you are normally offered a menu of options ranging from savings accounts to select bond and mutual funds.

Myth: You'll pay tax on your Roth IRA contributions when you withdraw money before retirement.

Fact: You don't pay taxes on withdrawals of your contributions from a Roth IRA, no matter the reason for withdrawal. But you could pay taxes and a penalty on earnings. However, the money is ordered. For instance, let's say you deposit $3,000 per year for 3 years. Now $9,000 is worth $10,000 with interest. If you withdraw up to $9,000, you won't owe income taxes on the withdrawal. However, if you withdraw $10,000, you would have to pay income taxes on just the $1,000 of interest plus a penalty, if you are under age 59½.

Myth: You get tax-free earnings if withdrawing funds for education.

Fact: The only way to avoid paying taxes on earnings withdrawn is if you keep the money in the account until you're 59½ and have held the money for 5 years. However, you won't pay the 10 percent withdrawal penalty on the earnings.

Myth: Small contributions won't add up.

Fact: You may consider saving with a few dollars, whether for college savings or retirement, and then look at a few months' accumulation and say "why bother?" But saving less than $100 per month at age 30 can add up to a few hundred thousand when you're ready for retirement. You may never use the money you saved in a Roth for your child's education because you saved in a 529 plan. Now, the extra money you saved in a Roth is extra retirement funding.

You don't have to risk of the rest of your financial life in order to save for your child's college education. Balance your and your child's needs. One of the best gifts you can give your child is making smart financial decisions and teaching them to do the same.

Chapter Wrap-Up

- $ You can always add more to your child's college savings later if you can afford to do so.

- $ You will still have to pay taxes on earnings from your accounts if you deposit the money in college savings later. Of course, once it's in a 529 plan account, it will grow federal- and often state-income-tax-free.

- $ Speak to a financial advisor at least once to discuss your overall financial life plans.

- $ When you invest money in an UTMA account, your child owns the account on their 18th birthday. Don't use this type of account if you want to remain in control or use it for purposes other than paying for your child's living expenses before they're 18.

- $ Be careful of overfunding UTMAs, because after $1,050 (the cap in 2015), they are taxed at the kiddie tax rate. After $2,100, they are taxed at the parents' tax rate.

- $ Roth IRAs allow families to withdraw money for college tuition penalty-free, but you will pay tax on earnings.

- $ Contributions to Roth IRAs aren't tax deductible, but the money does grow tax-free.

- Use a Roth IRA when you are unsure what the money will be used for, as you don't want to give up 529 plan state income tax contributions if you want to use the money for college savings.

- If you know you want to use the money for retirement, you may be better off investing in your company's 401K plan than in a Roth IRA, especially if there is a company matching program on all or part of your contributions.

Ways to Increase College Savings with the Help of Friends and Family

While it doesn't seem like I could dedicate a whole chapter just to asking friends and family for money for your child's education, I can.

Why? You need to know how to ask politely and at appropriate times. You also need to know how different websites (those from your college savings plan and those that help you save in general) work for college savings.

In this chapter, you also learn about rewards programs in which you, your friends, and your family can donate with rebates from online shopping and dining. Thus, you and your loved ones have an option to potentially contribute hundreds per year to your child's education without spending a dime.

By the time this chapter ends, you'll be able to start planning family contributions that can help you meet your college savings goals without completely emptying your savings and investment accounts. After all, my main reason for writing this book is to help you figure out how to help your child without hurting your long-term financial well-being.

Asking Politely for Money, Especially Around the Holidays

Asking for money as a gift can seem a bit tacky and sometimes cold, but it isn't. Grandparents have been giving their grandchildren U.S. savings bonds since before our parents were born. Parents are just getting savvier about it. They'll put gift codes or plan or registry gifting information on announcements for birthday parties, graduations, holidays, and other special events in their child's life. Announcements can be quite creative, with emailed themes and printed gift certificates.

In addition, children can have web pages on sites such as the Utah Education Savings Plan. You can select a plan in the state of Utah, no matter what state you live in. However, if you live in another state that has state income tax deductions for credits that require you to choose a specific plan, you should consider those, too. They will have gifting programs and often have printable gift certificates or greeting cards.

What about that gift code I mentioned? Let's say you don't want to give out your account number on an invitation. You just need a gift code that can be punched in on your plan's 529 plan website. Most plans have a way for you to request a code on their site. Plans that work with Ascensus accounts, for example, use a site called ugift.com for gifting. You can go directly to ugift.com or start on your plan's website. You then simply give the website and gift code information where you would put registry information, such as for a baby shower.

What if your family still considers a monetary gift a bit impersonal? After all, were you thrilled when your parents got you a savings bond instead of a Cabbage Patch doll, Tickle Me Elmo, or a Transformer? Probably not. So if a grandparent or someone close to you says, "I'd love to get your child a 529 plan gift, but I want to give them something fun." You can respond, "The 529 gift card helps a lot for the future, but you still can buy a small toy with it if you'd like." Especially for small children, recommend getting a small toy or a $10 gift card to a place where the child can purchase a toy.

Giftofcollege.com began selling college savings gift cards in retailers and grocery stores this year. The gift cards cost under $5 plus the amount of the card's value. They're redeemed at giftofcollege.com and then deposited into whatever 529 plan you have. The bonus to physical gift cards is your family can pick up a toy while they're there, so they'll have a fun, tangible gift to give to your child as well.

Giftofcollege.com also has a registry where you can set up a free profile, and family members can donate anytime. E-gifting this way will have a fee for the gifter, so it's better to give those expressing interest in giving more for college the code from your plan when they are ready to make a contribution.

For parties, you can send out invitations from the plan for free or use free or inexpensive electronic invitations from websites such as www.evite.com or www.paperlesspost.com. Both offer an array of invitation designs.

Of course, don't specify amounts for gifts. This is where asking for money is tacky. But there are other ways around specifying dollar amounts. The webpage states your child's goal so family members have an idea of how much you'll need to save for college and how close you are. Plus, think about this when receiving small monetary gifts: Every $10 gift that grows at 5 percent equals about $25 after 18 years. If you received ten $10 gift certificates at a baby shower, you've essentially saved $250 for your baby, with dozens of other gifting opportunities and occasions to come before your child heads off to college.

Free Rewards Programs

I like free money for college savings. Who doesn't? It's the kind of money you get for going about your daily life and suddenly money appears, kind of like tax credits for tuition you would have paid regardless of whether the IRS gave you $2,500 back. In the case of cash-back rebate and rewards programs, you would shop anyway, so why not earn money you wouldn't normally have earned?

Shopping programs come in two forms: general cash rebate programs and college savings–specific cash rebate programs. Most cash rebate programs you find online will offer you a percentage of what you spend on shopping online for clothes, electronics, travel bookings, sports equipment, and more. Others will allow rebates for restaurants and even home purchases.

Upromise, an education rebate program, deposits the money directly into your student loan or 529 plan account. When I use Upromise for my student loan repayment, I enter the product I want or the company I want to buy it from in the search box. Then I click on the site from there. A bonus: It also shows coupons available. For instance, when I buy office supplies, I'll check for coupon codes for Office Depot. You can find coupons by clicking on the Offers button on the Upromise site. I'll copy the coupon code before I head away from the site. As long as I click on the retailer website link from the Upromise website, I'll get a 5 percent rebate, or whatever's offered by that merchant, to put toward my student loan payments. Plus, I saved money on the product from the coupon code I used. Families can purchase discounted restaurant certificates through restaurant.com and get back a percentage for college savings, too.

Whichever program you choose to use, check its record on the Better Business Bureau website (www.bbb.org) to make sure the company you are thinking about choosing has few or no customer complaints.

Debunking Rewards Programs Myths for Upromise by Sallie Mae

Erin Condon, President of Upromise, shows you how you can get money toward paying off your student loans without spending a dime beyond your regular budget.

Myth: There must be a catch because retailers wouldn't want to help my child with college savings.

Fact: There is no catch. Over 850 participating online retailers (e.g., gap.com, barnesandnoble.com) give 5 percent cash back to Upromise members who are saving and paying for college when they start their online shopping at Upromise.com. Upromise MasterCard customers double that and earn 10 percent on online purchases through the Upromise shopping mall.

Myth: Upromise is only for helping families save for college.

Fact: While we encourage members to use some or all of their earned money for college, you can dip into the account and splurge. You can also diversify the rewards you earn. Some of our members automatically transfer a portion of their rewards cash to reduce or pay down their own Sallie Mae student loans while also putting away a portion for their child's education in a 529 plan. This way, you're paying for both your higher education as well as your child's. You can also request a check and use that money to apply to loans outside of Sallie Mae, such as a Federal Direct Loan.

Myth: You have to buy extra things that you don't need in order to rack up Upromise rewards.

Fact: You can spend the same amount you normally would, but by shopping with participating merchants you can collect meaningful money back for your student loans. With ship-to-store partners, members can buy online, pick up in store, and earn cash-back rewards. Additionally, there are everyday-essentials partners in the program like soap.com and diapers.com, where you can order everything from toiletries to food and have it shipped for free while earning cash back for college.

Benjamin joined Upromise in 2002, when he was single. He would start on the Upromise site when booking personal and work travel and doing his Christmas shopping. He also earned money back on groceries by registering his grocery rewards cards on the Upromise website.

Without spending an extra dime over what he normally would, he earned $600 per year. Four years later, he paid off his student loans. Then he started working with his new wife, Kimberly, to use Upromise rewards in addition to other budgeting strategies to pay off her student loans. In 2008, they welcomed their first child and began using Upromise to save for their children's education. They buy diapers, toilet paper, and cleaning products online. Their rewards per item doubled because they have the Upromise MasterCard. When Benjamin has a work pizza party, he goes to a pizza place that's signed up with Upromise's dining program and earns 10 percent of the cost for his children's college education. If he needs an item from a home improvement store, he orders online and picks up in store in order to get his Upromise rewards.

Kimberly and Benjamin earned $1,000 just last year for their children without affecting their budget. They are frugal in their day-to-day to lives. Spoiled groceries are a rarity. If they notice an item spoiling repeatedly, they think about why they buy it and determine whether they should buy less. Benjamin eats lunch out sometimes and brings lunch on other days. Kimberly teaches music at a local daycare and enjoys a huge discount on their children's preschool costs.

They still indulge occasionally and go skiing, but seldom wonder where a single penny went. They now have over $10,000 saved for college per child.

Myth: You can only earn Upromise rewards for online purchases.

Fact: Through Upromise dining partners, you can earn rewards as high as 8 percent when you go out to eat, and you can earn rewards on everything you do through the Upromise MasterCard. We also offer in-store cash-back rewards; just check our website for local participating stores. You can even get rewards when you buy or sell a home or book travel. Upromise has also expanded its local program; there are many opportunities to go to Upromise.com and click to activate in-store offers at local small businesses in your area.

Myth: You must have Sallie Mae loans to be a Upromise member.

Fact: Upromise offers Sallie Mae borrowers the ability to automatically transfer money to their student loan account on a monthly basis, but anyone who joins Upromise can get a check every month for the sum of their rewards when they have a balance of at least $10. With that check, they can make a payment toward their student loans or any type of debt. The check can also be deposited into any savings or checking account.

Credit Card Rewards

If your credit card offers a cash-back program, you could be earning cash right now that you could save for your child's college education. But there are major cautions and considerations when it comes to using credit cards for rewards:

- Only charge what you can reasonably pay off in the same month.

- Even if you pay off your credit cards in the same month, your credit score recognizes what your highest balance was for the month. Unless you are charging on your card for an actual emergency, always stay under 15 percent of your limit.

- Compare rates and cash-back programs among at least three credit cards. These could be three that you already have or three new ones you've found through research. Look at what the interest rate is if you plan on leaving charges on for more than a month. Find out if there is an annual fee and how cash-back rewards are earned. For example, cards may have different limits on how much of your charges can earn cash back. There could also be special bonus cash-back rewards for special purchases such as for gas and groceries. Compare offers before applying for new credit cards.

- Ask your bank about other rewards programs it might offer. Your bank may have a great rewards program you could switch to right now, and all it takes is one phone call.

Bottom line: Free money is good money. You can take advantage of these kinds of programs to pay off your loans faster without spending anything beyond what you would normally spend.

Case Studies in College Savings Gifting

Two Utah families in the same state have found ways to make gifting benefit their loved ones.

Mary is somewhat of a 529 plan Mrs. Santa. She saved for college and paid for her daughter's college education, and now she's saving in five accounts for friends and family. Her 529 brood includes two godsons, a grandniece, a grandnephew, and a friend's child.

She has no plans to pay for each child's full college education, but she funds each regularly on a system: $5 per month, $25 for birthdays, and $25 for Christmas. This base amount adds up to $110 annually per child. When one of the children accomplishes something fantastic like becoming an Eagle Scout, she'll add another $100. She figures the total she deposits will at least pay for textbooks.

Mary also helps organize 529 plan contributions among other friends and family members. For birthdays and holidays, she sends notifications containing the link that the Utah Education Savings Plan provides for families to send money to a particular account holder's account to each child's family members: parents, grandparents, aunts, and uncles. Some of the parents also contribute money. The accounts will easily add up to a few thousand dollars each for education by the time they're ready to be used.

Now let's look at Mickelle and Doug. They have three young children from age 12 weeks to 3 years old in a home crammed with toys, furniture, and clothing their children outgrow on a regular basis. Grandparents and friends love bringing giant pandas, toys with plastic lights, and anything that looks fun or impressive to the children at birthday parties. But with an overflowing closet of toys they have to rotate out every 2 weeks, they've asked grandparents to contribute to their childrens' college education accounts instead. The grandparents love the idea and are generally relieved to not have to think about what to give their grandchildren.

Mickelle and Doug are also budget conscious and contribute to their children's college savings investment accounts without sacrificing their savings.

Their secret? They have one car and live a simple lifestyle. The children love riding the train around town, and they don't take a lot of vacations. "Why go to Disneyland when we can have fun everyday?" Mickelle says.

Going to breakfast on the weekend is one of the family's favorite treats. They live in a relatively small house compared to their friends, but they also live close to downtown Salt Lake City, so they always have inexpensive things to do without the need for two cars. Everything in their life is prioritized by their wants and needs.

LESSONS FROM CASE STUDIES

- Small donations add up.

- Send out links from your college savings plan to relatives. It makes their lives easier to know what to buy your child.

- An organizer role is as important as funding. You can do a lot for your family or friends by opening an account and sending out notices for others to donate, even if you can't afford to donate much yourself.

- College savings gifts are as fun as giant pandas, especially if your closet is already overflowing with toys.

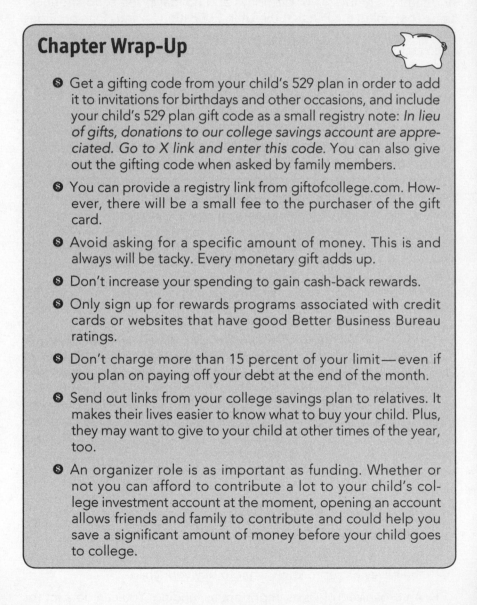

Chapter Wrap-Up

⑤ Get a gifting code from your child's 529 plan in order to add it to invitations for birthdays and other occasions, and include your child's 529 plan gift code as a small registry note: *In lieu of gifts, donations to our college savings account are appreciated. Go to X link and enter this code.* You can also give out the gifting code when asked by family members.

⑤ You can provide a registry link from giftofcollege.com. However, there will be a small fee to the purchaser of the gift card.

⑤ Avoid asking for a specific amount of money. This is and always will be tacky. Every monetary gift adds up.

⑤ Don't increase your spending to gain cash-back rewards.

⑤ Only sign up for rewards programs associated with credit cards or websites that have good Better Business Bureau ratings.

⑤ Don't charge more than 15 percent of your limit—even if you plan on paying off your debt at the end of the month.

⑤ Send out links from your college savings plan to relatives. It makes their lives easier to know what to buy your child. Plus, they may want to give to your child at other times of the year, too.

⑤ An organizer role is as important as funding. Whether or not you can afford to contribute a lot to your child's college investment account at the moment, opening an account allows friends and family to contribute and could help you save a significant amount of money before your child goes to college.

Last-Minute Savings Boosts:
For Parents of High Schoolers

- Chapter 5: Savings Strategies: Finding "Free" Money
- Chapter 6: Ways Your Teen Can Help
- Chapter 7: Scholarship Application Strategies Throughout High School
- Chapter 8: Comparing Schools Through College Visits and Financial Aid Award Letters

This section is geared toward parents of high schoolers. It teaches them about different ways to increase savings and how to make savvy decisions on scholarships, school choice, and career exploration. One of my favorite parts of this section is about budgeting in college as well as comparing financial aid letters in chapter 8 and the FAFSA in chapter 7. Parents with college students will want to check out this chapter, too. Since the FAFSA form is filled out each year and financial aid award letters are also received annually, these are also great chapters for parents of college students. Chapter 6, which covers career exploration, is valuable for parents of children of all ages.

Savings Strategies: Finding "Free" Money

When you look at the price of college today, it may seem like you'll never be able to afford to pay for your child's education based on your current savings. However, whether you've saved $5 or $25,000, there's still time to increase what you have. Families can continue saving and contributing throughout college.

In Section II, I discuss last-minute strategies for saving, your teen's contributions, scholarships, and school selection. I start this chapter with ways to give your college savings a quick boost with "free" money from state 529 plan scholarships, matching grants, tax deductions and credits, and more. The goal isn't to fund your child's education completely, but rather to contribute what you can.

Last-Minute Savings

Let's start with looking at a few myths about last-minute savings.

Debunking Myths About Last-Minute Savings

New York–based certified financial planner Stacy Francis busts a few myths about last-minute college savings.

Myth: It's too late to start saving.

Fact: It's never too late to start saving. There are a lot of ways to ramp up the savings in that 2- to 3-year window before college starts. For instance, the "we are family strategy": Open up a 529 plan, if you don't already have one, and let all relatives and dear friends know that instead of gifts for holidays, special occasions, or birthdays, you'd rather your child receive money for their college savings plan. I know one woman who did this, and she received $3,500 outside savings from graduation presents for her son. The money paid for college expenses the family hadn't planned for such as textbooks and a laptop.

Myth: There's no time left for money to grow.

Fact: Your child will be in college for 4 years. Therefore, if you start investing in their freshman year of high school, that money has 7 years to increase in value before your child becomes a senior in college. Your investments will gradually get safer as you switch to investments with less risk, but it will still grow much faster than stuffing money in your mattress or not investing at all. Plus, you can still get state tax deductions or credits.

Myth: You can't continue to save while your student's in college.

Fact: Not only is it possible, but it's a good idea for both you and your child to continue setting aside money for college. If your teen has a part-time job, at least part of the money should be used for tuition or necessary expenses.

Myth: All education debt is good debt.

Fact: You will have to pay these loans back, so don't borrow $100,000 to $200,000 for your child's undergraduate education. Be reasonable.

Myth: Once you pass a deadline, your child is out of luck for getting a scholarship.

Fact: There are a variety of scholarships and grants with different deadlines. I had a client who got into Harvard and couldn't afford it after her mother lost her job. The student worked for months to find scholarship information and ended up with a full-ride scholarship to USC. Not everyone will get a full-ride scholarship, but most individuals who work hard at researching and applying for scholarships will find some degree of grant or scholarship aid.

Myth: Small amounts add up.

Fact: You can't change your mortgage and rent immediately, but you can change the money that seeps out of your pocket. Are you buying too many lattes? Do you love shopping and going out to lunch afterward? If you can switch from a $20 lunch to a $10 lunch once a week and then skip one latte, you can add $14 a week to college savings. Over the course of a year, that's enough for several textbooks. You could multiply these savings if other members of your family also gave up one item per week.

WHAT YOU NEED TO KNOW ABOUT LAST-MINUTE SAVINGS

- You don't have to do it yourself. Family and friends may contribute money for graduations, holidays, birthdays, and other special occasions.

- Cutting just one or two small items from your budget each month while your child is in high school can add up to enough to pay for textbooks.

- Paying for college is a family project. Include your teen in the process. Any scholarship he or she wins is a dollar the family doesn't have to come up with.

- Your money still has time to grow. Your investments have 7 years to grow before your first-year high school student becomes a senior in college.

Extra Help from Your State

Your state tax office and your 529 plan might be two of your closest allies when saving for college.

STATE 529 PLAN SCHOLARSHIPS

529 plan scholarships are awarded in quite a few states, but who qualifies and what is the difference between a 529 plan scholarship and a regular one? A 529 scholarship is different than a normal scholarship in that the money must be deposited into your 529 plan, but this is a good thing. After all, you want that money to get invested and grow. A $5,000 scholarship earned by your child as a first-year high school student can increase in value to over $6,000 before it's needed for the first-year of college if the money earns a 5 percent rate of return. Even a $500 scholarship could give you a $600 savings boost.

How does my child qualify? It depends on the state. In Maine, scholarships are awarded based on financial need after filling out the FAFSA when your child is ready for college. In Colorado, the scholarship is based on financial need, but you do have to apply. In Maine, Missouri, Nevada, and Ohio, a great essay written by your child could earn extra college savings. Missouri also has a fun scholarship sponsored by a local zoo that includes an annual zoo membership. Sometimes scholarships are awarded by randomly selecting entrants or even by entrants mentioning the plan on social media.

How do you find out whether your state offers a 529 plan scholarship or even multiple scholarship options? Check your plan's website. However, you can miss details on websites occasionally. I recommend that you call your 529 plan, too, to ask. It never hurts to use more than one method of communication. Plus, you want to make sure you know all the rules and that your child applies in the correct way.

Is there a time of year when 529 plan scholarships are more prevalent? For 529 plans, May 29 is practically a national college savings holiday! Initiation fees might be waived on prepaid tuition plans during this time period. You could see a slew of $529 scholarships offered.

Other deadlines can be throughout the year. For instance, one scholarship could have a July deadline, while another has a deadline in February.

AGE LIMITS FOR MATCHING GRANTS

The good news is if you continue to save for your child's education while he or she is in college, you could still qualify for matching grants in many states. Matching grants are programs that some states have in which they match your contribution by percentages up to 200 percent. Check www.collegesavings.org to see if your state has a matching grants program. You can read more about them in chapter 2 (pages 18-19).

But matching grants often have age limits for enrollment and eligible final contributions. For example, in Arkansas you can still get matching grants for your child up to their 24th birthday as long as they started getting matching grants before their 19th birthday. In Louisiana, age is not a factor at all. Check with your state plan for the rules regarding matching grants programs.

Tax Deductions and Credits

I talk about state tax deductions and credits in previous chapters, but they also have to be a part of last-minute savings strategies. For example, if you saved $100 per month in a college investment plan and your income tax rate is 5 percent, you'd reduce your state income taxes by $60 per year. In 7 years, you'd accrue $420. In 8 years, you'd accrue $480. Not bad for a bit of extra funding.

A fun tip: The money you earn through Upromise rewards also qualifies for state income tax deductions. Make sure you look at your 529 plan statement at the end of the year to see how much came from contributions. Then subtract money that was donated by family members. To learn more about the Upromise rewards program for online shopping and retail purchases, see chapter 4.

Note: In most cases, you can't get a tax deduction on money donated directly to your 529 plan by relatives. So if a family member made a donation to your account, they can take the tax credit in a state that allows tax deductions for contributions made by anyone versus solely by the child's parent or legal guardian.

The biggest caution at this stage when it comes to state income tax deductions and credits is to be careful about transferring 529 plan funds from one state plan to another. Why would you do that and what is the penalty? Let's say you moved from Nebraska to New York and want to participate in a New York's 529 plan instead. So you roll all the money you had saved for your child in Nebraska into your plan in New York. Nebraska could ask for all the tax deductions or credits back because you switched plans. Unless you've checked with your state treasurer's office and the plan, and seen in writing that your tax benefits won't be recaptured, leave the money in your old plan and start a new one. You can have multiple plans for one child, and the money can be used for any accredited higher education institution, no matter in which state or country it's located.

Ramping Up Savings

Just because your teen is within a few years of college doesn't mean it's time to start digging into your savings account or Roth IRA, unless your financial advisor says you're financially able to do so.

Here are a few more tips for saving during those last few years, including during the first 3 years of college:

- **Make college savings a monthly bill.** Automatic savings, even $25 per month, deposited into a 529 plan can make you feel like you're doing your part, and then you can forget about it the rest of the year if you choose to do so. This $300 per year saved for 8 years adds up to $2,400 without any earnings. However, if you started saving $25 when your child was a baby, and you can now comfortably afford to deposit $200 a month, ramp it up.

- **Review rewards programs and cash-back credit card information from chapter 4.** Think about Benjamin and Kimberly who were able to accrue $1,000 in Upromise rewards last year from online shopping, restaurant purchases, and credit card rewards. They didn't spend an extra dime beyond their normal budget. Eight years of rewards adds $8,000 to their children's funds. Plus, the contribution could qualify for state tax deductions.

- **Become the CEO of your child's college fund with your teen as the VP.** This means that you are discussing with your child on a regular basis how you can afford to contribute and your overall strategy for paying for college. If your child understands finances, they may be a little more diligent about finding an affordable college or applying for scholarships.

  In the next few chapters, I talk about the aspects of paying for college beyond savings, such as part-time employment and dedicated scholarship searches. I also talk about community college and AP courses taken during high school to reduce overall student loan debt.

- **Set aside time to help your child academically and with scholarship searches.** The most valuable education I received before college was my father teaching me how to do math in my head. The lessons he taught me got me through algebra, my MBA program, and eventually were part of the reason I was able to write this book. I talk about a family effort for scholarship searches in chapter 7, but helping your child get good grades is an excellent start. Spending a few dollars on tutoring to improve grades in subject areas where you can't help can also boost your child's college acceptance and scholarship chances.

- **Redo the budget review you did in chapter 1 (pages 5–7).** Every budget needs a little sprucing. Go back to chapter 1 and look over ways you can painlessly cut your budget. However, getting deeper into your budget with a budgeting cleanse is also helpful once in a while. When you give up spending money on entertainment or dining out for a few weeks, you can show your child how to save money and still enjoy themselves. Deposit the money you would have spent in a piggy bank or a clear glass jar your child can see. Challenge your child to do the same, but don't force it. Let them know for every dollar they save from their allowance, you'll match it for their college fund.

  Michelle Singletary, my budgeting hero and author of *The 21-Day Financial Fast*, goes back to a bare-bones budget every year for 3 weeks to pinpoint areas in which she can improve. She realized that she and her husband were eating out too much on the road. She started eating more fruits and veggies while traveling and trimmed her budget a bit. I did the financial fast recently: I realized I was buying too many coffees and meals out that I enjoyed less than cooking at home. Now, I eat out less, but still enjoy coffee with friends and dinner out once or twice weekly. Not only did this equivocate to savings, but I lost 5 pounds, and I feel much healthier.

- **Know that it's not too late to save your pennies.** What's great about the piggy bank method of saving the change from purchases is that now you can have your high schooler participate. Put your teen on a cash budget. The change goes into a piggy bank. At the end of the week, add your change to theirs. You'll be surprised at how much money piles up. I've seen families save a couple hundred dollars per year this way.

Chapter Wrap-Up

- Your money still has time to grow. Your investments have 7 years to grow before your first-year high school student becomes a senior in college.

- Take advantage of opportunities for free money from your state such as 529 plan scholarships and state income tax benefits.

- Check with your state plan for the rules regarding matching grants programs.

- File amended returns to collect tax benefits you forgot to claim in previous years.

- Cutting just one or two small items from your budget each month while your child is in high school can add up to enough to pay for textbooks.

- Your teen can help, too. Besides work, any scholarship he or she wins is a dollar the family doesn't have to come up with.

- Contribute to your teen's success by helping with homework or hiring a tutor when needed. Academic success in high school will increase your child's chances of being accepted to a college and receiving a scholarship.

- Find small ways to increase your savings without hurting your budget. Only increase your contributions if you can afford to do so.

Ways Your Teen Can Help

Your teen will feel more invested in paying for college and the college selection process if they contribute in ways that have a direct financial impact and that increase scholarship and employment opportunities during and after college. Some of the ways your teen can contribute are part-time jobs, shadow days, internships, and focusing on academics. In this chapter, I talk about the various considerations of getting a job and how to make sure that work experience benefits your teen's future, possibly even influencing their career path. Shadow days and internships are great ways to explore career options. I also cover the benefits of your teen treating school as their job.

Teens Contributing Through Part-Time Jobs

Getting a part-time job in high school contributes more than just money to a teen's future. If your teen contributes financially to their education, they will feel more invested in the college selection process and in their future success. They'll also gain experience that could help them pick majors, commit to a career choice, and get a job after they graduate from college.

FIGURING OUT HOW MUCH TIME YOUR TEEN SHOULD DEVOTE TO WORKING

Figuring out the time schedule for your teen is probably one of the most crucial parts of work experience. Why? First off, if your teen sacrifices their time spent on schoolwork to pay for college, they could miss out on valuable scholarships because they didn't focus enough on academics. In addition to academic performance, extracurricular activities such as sports, debate team, and drama club can impact scholarships as well. This is why many teens end up working during the summer when school and activities schedules aren't as hectic.

To see if your teen has the time available to work, sit down with them and discuss a time budget. For instance, if they get home at 3 p.m., how much time is generally spent on homework? How much time do they need for extracurricular activities? Could they work a few hours on the weekends, or do extracurricular activities interfere with this possibility? Some families may decide working should be saved for the summer when high schoolers can balance work with a social life.

Shadow Days and Initial Career Exploration

Changing majors multiple times or returning to school because you didn't like the career you trained for the first time makes college even more expensive. Thus, your first task in paying for college is career exploration.

Even if your teen has known what they wanted to do since they were 5, they still need to solidify their career goals with shadow days, volunteer work, and/or internships. A shadow day is when your child spends the day with someone who works in the career field they want to enter. Generally, your child will spend a partial workday with the professional they are shadowing and ask them questions about what their job is like. You'd be surprised how willing professionals are to open up to them.

When I was pursuing my master's degree, I called up the human resources department of one of the most respected magazines in my state. Within a day, I had an appointment to chat with one of the senior editors about what a career in magazine journalism is like. Being a student is powerful. There are journalists who've worked in the field for 20 years who couldn't get the same appointment. While I recommend also completing internships, shadow days are a quick way for a high school senior in the midst of college application or admissions season to learn about a career.

If your teen doesn't know what they want to do, shadow days are still a good practice. They just may want to try a wider variety of career fields based on their interests and talents. If your teen is not sure how to translate their interests and talents into a paying job, they should chat with their school counselor.

What else can high school students do to learn about career possibilities? Julie Hartline, a former American School Counselor Association (ASCA) National School Counselor of the Year recipient, has students take interest inventories and assessments so she can better match them with careers and assess their likes and dislikes. The interest inventories and assessments include statements such as *I like to work outdoors.* and *I like to draw.* Based on the student's responses, career clusters are recommended for further exploration.

"I discourage them from picking careers based on income alone and always ask how many of them know someone who hates their job," says Hartline. "I explain how important it is to like what you have to do every day! Additionally, it is important for them to look at projected growth of careers and salary information in this economic climate. They do not want to spend 4 years in college, only to be unable to find a job in their field of study."

Reach Out to Your Teen's School Counselor

If you haven't met your teen's high school counselor, you may be in for a shock. School counseling used to be a less formal occupation. My counselor was the football coach, and none of my friends remember their high school counselor as being the one who helped them make important decisions. I didn't learn anything about career exploration from mine. Now, high school counselors have master's degrees, send out scholarship newsletters, and can help guide your children. Set up an appointment to meet your teen's counselor. You may be pleasantly surprised.

Finding Career-Focused Jobs and Internships

If your teen is pursuing a part-time job, why not have it be one that helps them figure out their career path? For instance, even a job as a cashier in a retail shop of a hospital might be a great place for them to learn about the medical profession.

Also, have them make inquiries about free or paid internships at places they'd want to work after college.

Finally, make sure your teen discuss with their high school counselor where they'd like to work. The counselor may be able to make job recommendations that will help them solidify their career choices. Perhaps your child will end up doing a paid job during the summer and then internships or shadow days during the school year.

How much can your child contribute to their education from working for one summer? Here's an example: Let's say your child worked for 10 weeks full time (40 hours a week) for two summers at the federal minimum wage of $7.25. They'd earn $2,900 each summer, totaling $5,800 (before taxes). That's about two-thirds of the average annual fees at a public 4-year institution for the 2014–2015 school year, according to the College Board's Trends in College Pricing (http://trends.collegeboard.org/college-pricing).

Note: The minimum wage is a bit higher in a little over half of the 50 states. (You can find the minimum wage for your state at www.dol.gov/whd/minwage/america.htm.)

Then if your child does an internship during the year, they'll save money on tuition by being more sure of their major. As I said earlier, students are less likely to change majors if they've had exposure to different career options.

You and/or their guidance counselor should help your teen to create a skills-based resume and practice interview skills with them. Remind them to wear professional attire, generally business casual, to interviews.

School as a Job

Your teen can help with college expenses through a variety of ways of earning college credit during high school. It's not unusual for high schools to offer the opportunity to earn credit by taking a test to earn advanced placement credit after completing the course, but some high schools also offer dual credit programs. Taking community college courses while still in high school is another option for your teen.

AP Exams: The fee for an AP (Advanced Placement) exam in 2015 is $91. The number of college credits earned varies; it's up to each individual school to decide how much credit they'll award for a score. For example, one school may award 3 credits for an AP score, while another awards 6 credits in that subject area. Six credits of tuition could translate to thousands of dollars. If your child is able to test out of 12 credits of courses, they've essentially saved at least the same amount of money they would have earned working at a summer job for minimum wage.

Dual Credit Programs: It's a growing trend for high schools to offer dual credit programs, in which students take college courses on their high school campus that are developed by local community colleges.

Is there a catch to earning college credits in high school? Earning credit in English, science, or math generally is a good idea. After all, these courses are pretty standard in any college's core. However, one college or major at that institution may require statistics while another requires calculus, for example. Before your teen starts debating which courses they should take, they should be in touch with their top six school choices' admissions department to see what kind of credits and scores they accept as transfer credits.

Community College Courses: The final way to earn college credits while still in high school is to take community college courses over the summer or maybe even an additional course at a community college during the school year.

Taking community college courses (although I did so after I was out of high school) saved me thousands on my MBA. How? I was required to take 12 credits of business courses before I began the regular curriculum because I wasn't a business major as an undergraduate.

But if your child takes community college courses, should they forego work experience? No. They can still do shadow days. Shadow days only take a couple of hours, and they can shadow five or more individuals in different professions. Set up a career exploration schedule in a joint meeting with your child and their school counselor. This schedule may include college courses during the summer, then shadow days in the fall and an internship in the spring.

Huge Tuition Saver

In the 10 years I've been writing about education and saving money, community college guaranteed transfer programs have absolutely become one of my favorite cost-saving measures.

Here's how they work: Let's say your child wants a degree from the University of California, Berkeley. They should look at California community colleges in the Bay Area and see which schools have guaranteed transfer agreements with UC Berkley. Then they can attend their first 2 years of school at a much cheaper rate and still get their degree from the school they want. Even better—if the community college accepts your child's AP credits, they can graduate much faster, maybe in a year or less, with their associate's degree before moving on to their dream school.

Note: Have your child apply to UC Berkeley, too. It doesn't hurt students to apply to their dream schools because they could get a full scholarship.

With the three approaches above, career exploration is still in the schedule with shadow days, and no extracurricular activities that are helpful for scholarship planning were dropped.

Case Study in School as a Job: Janae and Randy

Janae and Randy were just thinking about how their daughters never had traditional summer jobs as teenagers. From the time they were in elementary school, the girls were working their way toward college. All their kids were taught the importance of writing skills, which helped them win multiple essay contests. Their middle child, Morgan, started off the spree of essay contest winnings for the girls by writing a story about her blanket being comforting like a blanket and a mom rolled into one. The essay won her $1,000 from Mimi's Café at age 6.

Amber, their oldest daughter, followed suit by not just winning essay contests, but winning a slew of academic, leadership, and community service scholarships. Now in college, Amber has enough scholarships that the $2,000 her parents put in her 529 plan when she was younger isn't really needed. But the mentorship she had in Girl Scouts has proven invaluable.

Through a woman she met in Girl Scouts, Amber was able to help a school that couldn't afford to start a science and math academy.

The girls' dad, Randy, reminded Amber annually about the scholarship offered through his work. When it was time to apply, she won $5,000 that renews every year.

Janae kept a binder of scholarships she'd heard about from other parents, the high school counselors, and even in the magazine *Costco Connection*. She organized family meetings with the girls' school counselors every year but stays in touch five times per year. She discusses career exploration with her girls, too. The girls are constantly exposed to a variety of successful women taking different career paths.

The girls always knew they had to pay for their own educations, but they had the backing and support of their parents helping them find scholarships and encouraging academics. Janae and Randy bought Amber an ACT prep course, but then went with a cheaper tutor for their youngest, Megan, to improve her math skills.

"We want our kids to be happy," Janae says, "which only comes from building confidence in who they are and what they can achieve. We think their educations will help them achieve that happiness."

LESSONS FROM THE CASE STUDY

- Creating financially savvy kids begins when they're young. Janae and Randy's kids knew their goals from the beginning.

- Although Janae and Randy only contributed $2,000 to their oldest daughter's education, the equivalent of less than $10 per month for 18 years, they helped their children succeed by providing for them academically and helping them find scholarships. If Janae and Randy had provided more money instead, Amber would probably have student loans to make up the difference.

- Make appointments with high school counselors as early as eighth grade. Have a focused search and chat with other parents about their strategies.

- Nip academic problems in the bud. Megan needed math tutoring, which was much cheaper than ACT or SAT prep courses, to do well in school and on tests.

- Scholarship opportunities are everywhere. Keep your eyes and ears open to find them.

Chapter Wrap-Up

- Part-time and summer employment can help your child gain money for college and valuable work experience. Make sure they balance work with time needed for their studies and extracurricular activities.

- No matter whether your child is 14 or 18, you need to work with them on career exploration.

- Shadow days are a valuable resource as your teen explores their career choices. They can lead to further career exploration such as internships and part-time jobs.

- Teach your child research skills for both jobs and scholarships. In the job arena, a phone call to human resources is still as important as sending an electronic application.

- Schedule a family meeting with your teen's high school counselor. You need a community effort for finding scholarships and creating a path to success in school and beyond.

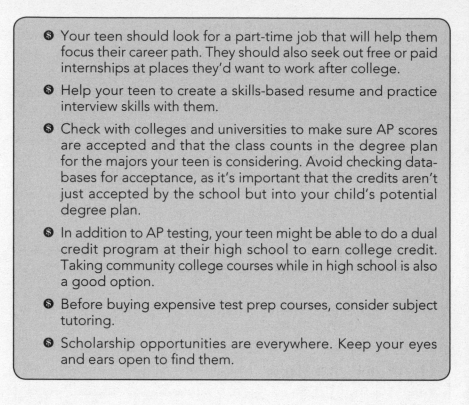

- Your teen should look for a part-time job that will help them focus their career path. They should also seek out free or paid internships at places they'd want to work after college.

- Help your teen to create a skills-based resume and practice interview skills with them.

- Check with colleges and universities to make sure AP scores are accepted and that the class counts in the degree plan for the majors your teen is considering. Avoid checking databases for acceptance, as it's important that the credits aren't just accepted by the school but into your child's potential degree plan.

- In addition to AP testing, your teen might be able to do a dual credit program at their high school to earn college credit. Taking community college courses while in high school is also a good option.

- Before buying expensive test prep courses, consider subject tutoring.

- Scholarship opportunities are everywhere. Keep your eyes and ears open to find them.

Scholarship Application Strategies Throughout High School

If there's one secret to paying for college and getting the most financial aid possible, it is this: The earlier you start, the better.

The good news is that when it comes to earning scholarships, every year of high school is a perfect time to prepare. So if you don't have a lot in college savings, or even if you do, this is your chapter. In it, I cover strategies for getting the most scholarship money possible and getting a ballpark estimate of what college costs early.

While it's best to begin research as a freshman, seniors can still boost their chances of finding scholarship money by filling out the Free Application for Federal Student Aid (FAFSA) form as soon as possible.

Avoid Making Big Financial Aid Mistakes

Let's begin by looking at a few myths about scholarships and financial aid.

Debunking Scholarship and Financial Aid Myths

Julie Hartline, 2009 American School Counselor Association School Counselor of the Year and Cobb County School District School Counseling and Advisement Consultant busts the most common myths about financial aid.

Myth: Filling out the FAFSA form is all parents need to do to get school scholarships and state and federal funding.

Fact: Schools often have more scholarships that you haven't automatically applied for by filling out the FAFSA, such as academic department scholarships. All students should call financial aid offices at universities to which they're considering applying to ask about scholarship availability, eligibility, and deadlines. Also, ask either the financial aid office or your school counselor about state deadlines for grants you might be able to receive.

Myth: You have to pay for assistance in finding scholarship information.

Fact: You can pay to have someone do the legwork of finding scholarships, but you can find scholarships on your own. A couple of good national websites on which students can search for scholarships are www.collegeweeklive.com and www.collegeboard.org. "Counselors often provide scholarship newsletters and share the websites that are available to assist in the process," says Hartline. "Additionally, counselors often contact students about specific scholarships that are good matches."

Myth: Your high school counselor doesn't help you.

Fact: Even at high schools where counselors are severely time-strapped due to other responsibilities, they will still help those who contact them with information on local and national scholarships. Set a family appointment with your student's high school counselor as early as possible.

Myth: The FAFSA deadline is the scholarship deadline, or scholarship deadlines are the same for all schools.

Fact: Every school and every scholarship can have different scholarship deadlines. You can look for scholarships year-round.

Myth: Apply for all scholarships you can find.

Fact: Scholarships that ask for a Social Security or account number may not be legitimate. If you suspect a scholarship may not be real, have your child bring all the information you have on it to their high school counselor before considering applying.

Myth: All scholarships are online.

Fact: I've had more than one student call a school's financial aid office, and magically there's additional aid. Remember your student's talents in addition to their GPA. There's a reason why the school accepted your teen. Give them the chance to offer more money. Plus, many scholarships are offered through local communities. Your high school counselor can provide information on these.

Myth: All scholarships are for high school seniors.

Fact: Students can apply for certain scholarships as early as their sophomore year in high school and as late as their senior year of college and beyond for graduate school. Research should begin during the freshman year of high school so you don't accidentally disqualify yourself from a scholarship you otherwise would have received. I've seen students fail to get a scholarship because they missed a requirement as simple as taking one art class.

Scholarship Application Timeline

There are different actions your child should take as they progress through high school, but if they haven't begun to search yet, they should review the steps I outline below in "Freshman and Sophomore Years" before moving on to further steps.

Before doing anything else, you should designate a place where your family can keep track of events. You can use a paper organizer or an electronic organizer such as Outlook or Google calendars.

The calendar should have deadlines for scholarships, signing up for classes, AP exams, and college applications. Also include any kind of career exploration activities. Always set 2-week reminders so deadlines don't sneak up on you.

Set aside time every few weeks to talk to your child about what steps they need to take to make themselves the best scholarship and college admissions candidate they can be. Then do as Janae and Randy did (see their case study in chapter 6) and start meeting with your child's high school counselor on an annual basis and communicating with them a few times throughout the school year.

FRESHMAN AND SOPHOMORE YEARS

The most important thing you can do when it comes to paying for college is to have a game plan that includes both looking for money for college and making sure your child is making informed decisions about school choices and career paths.

Set up a family meeting with your child's high school counselor. This is a great time to discuss what your child will need to do to become a great scholarship and college candidate. The path may include taking specific courses and should always include career exploration, which you can learn about in chapter 6.

Note: While school-specific scholarships aren't going to happen this early, some community scholarships will. Discuss with your child's high school counselor what scholarships they can start applying for now as well as those they can prepare to apply for in their junior or senior year.

In this initial meeting, make sure that you discuss grades and start looking for scholarships. This is also a good time to learn how to use net price calculators.

Net price calculators are calculators required by the Department of Education on school websites. They are one of the best tools families have for figuring out actual costs for their child to attend a school. Getting an idea early on of what schools cost will help parents and teens plan scholarship applications and college costs. Plus, the more information your teen has, the more they can accomplish in their school and career exploration.

Why can't they just look at the listed price of tuition? The sticker price of tuition is the scary number that may be really high at a fancy private school and generally a lot lower at a state school. For instance, according to the College Board's Trends in College Pricing (http://trends.collegeboard.org/college-pricing), the 2014–2015 private non-profit average tuition price was over three times the average cost of a public 4-year university's in-state tuition: $31,000 compared to $9,000. However, if a private school offers a lot of endowment money, your child could pay less or even nothing at the private school.

So how do you figure this out? Start by playing with net price calculators on different college websites. Enter your child's GPA (enter a higher GPA in case grades change) and family income. The higher GPA should be one the student could reasonably achieve. For instance, you can compare the difference in aid received if your B student bumped up to a B+ average. Check out netpricecalculator.collegeboard.org or www.usnews.com/education/best-colleges/features/net-price-calculator for large lists of net price calculators. Or you can do a simple Internet search for the school you're interested in.

JUNIOR YEAR

In a student's junior year, there are a slew of community and private scholarships available. Janae and Randy's oldest daughter earned one at this time. I earned a community service scholarship in my junior year, too.

Look for scholarship opportunities at your workplace, get information from your child's high school counselor, and check web-based scholarship databases. Add application deadlines to your calendar.

Don't send similar essays with every scholarship application. Your teen needs to get whatever information they can about what the company or nonprofit organization is looking for in winners. You can normally find information on what past winners did to earn the scholarship on the company or organization's website, as well as clues in the scholarship description. A scholarship essay that isn't tailored to the specific award isn't worth submitting.

This is also a great time to meet with the high school counselor again to revisit where your student needs to be grade- and activity-wise for maximum scholarship potential. Don't forget to revisit career exploration, too. Career exploration is important every year. So is getting tutoring when needed to improve admissions test scores and grades.

SENIOR YEAR

Now's the time to start thinking seriously about college choices. I talk more about this in the next chapter, but I want you start with the ideas that Julie Hartline outlines below.

Hartline recommends teens pick four to six colleges with one to two safety schools that are their backups, two to three target schools, and even one reach school (a school where your student may not have as a high of a GPA or college acceptance scores as the average admitted student). Her best tips for applying for college are as follows:

- Pick target schools where last year's freshmen GPAs and test scores match yours, as well as a backup school.

- Visit schools if you can, and listen to your gut. If you don't like the school on a visit, you will not like it 24/7.

- Know your deadlines and submit applications early. Don't wait until the last minute to ask for recommendations or request transcripts.

- Find schools that match your needs—location, size, sports, activities, majors—the things that make a difference in your life.

- Don't rule a school out because you think it will cost too much.

Senior year is also when students will fill out the FAFSA for the first time. Unfortunately, many families make mistakes when filling out the application that could cost their child thousands of dollars in free money. I've included a popular article from my forbes.com column on FAFSA mistakes on the pages that follow.

Avoiding FAFSA Mistakes

When filling out the FAFSA, many families make mistakes that could cause them to miss out on financial aid opportunities. In my article below, which originally appeared on forbes.com, I describe five costly mistakes that can cause you to miss out on thousands of dollars of free money for your child's college education. Read on to avoid missing out on free college dollars!

Five Costly Mistakes to Avoid When Filling Out the FAFSA

Filling out the Free Application for Federal Student Aid (FAFSA) is the single most important thing most families can do to get last-minute college funding help. That's why over 20 million people filled it out last year. However, there are big mistakes families can make that can cost them oodles of money.

These are five of the most costly mistakes families can make regarding the FAFSA:

1. Not filling it out.

Families who have decided that they don't want to fill out the FAFSA because they think it's the fast track to student loan borrowing may cause themselves to get into more debt to pay for their children's college education. Why? The information contained in FAFSA is sent to schools and is often used to help determine need-based scholarships and state and university grant eligibility. Not filling out the FAFSA is basically telling colleges and universities, "I'd rather pay for college by myself, thank you."

2. Not paying attention to the time frame.

Scholarships have deadlines, but also some financial aid such as university and state grants may be awarded on a first-come, first-serve basis among those who qualify. The FAFSA season begins on January 1. However, you can apply or make changes such as changing school picks later. At least your information will have already been processed by the federal government. Also, remember you won't have the previous year's tax information at the beginning of the year, so estimate it. If you fill out the FAFSA later in the year, there is an auto-fill-in option on the form to download IRS information.

Time frame is important for renewal FAFSAs for continuing college students, too.

3. Naming schools in the wrong order or not at all.

According to Martha Holler, spokesperson for Sallie Mae, you could miss out on state aid such as grants if you don't name state schools first in the list of schools you'd like to receive your financial information. Whether the order makes a difference in your state varies, but it's better to err on the side of caution and list state schools you're considering first. This doesn't mean private schools on your list will review your numbers any differently. The order won't matter to the individual schools you picked at all.

4. Closing out the confirmation page before reading it.

Your Expected Family Contribution, the number that may determine how much aid you'll receive, will be forwarded to you by email after completing the form. However, DON'T CLOSE OUT THE CONFIRMATION PAGE BEFORE READING IT FULLY! Why? According to Holler, the confirmation page contains important information on the schools you picked to receive your financial information, including graduation rates, transfer rates, and retention rates. Plus, there are links to fill out additional information for other children and additional forms that may be required by your state. Open links in new tabs if you need to click on more than one link.

5. Not making adjustments.

If you change your mind about which schools you're applying to, log back in to the FAFSA site and change your school information. You don't want to miss out on scholarships, grants, or other financial aid simply because you didn't list the school you'll actually attend. If your family income drops, this information needs to be amended on the form, too. If it's too late to amend income information on the FAFSA, you can make changes at the school by filling out a special circumstances form.

This article originally appeared on forbes.com.

More Tips on Scholarships and Other Sources of Funding

When your child applies for scholarships, the most important concept for them to remember is finding a good match. It doesn't help them to apply for 50 scholarships that don't match their special talents and interests. They're better off applying for 10 that they have a good chance of receiving.

Look at your own network. Ask the human resources department at your workplace about scholarships available to employees' children. One of my friends has parents who work for the same company. She won the company scholarship one year; years later, her brother won the scholarship. Your teen's part-time job may offer a scholarship program as well, so encourage them to inquire with human resources.

Every dollar earned is a dollar less of student debt. Just be careful to not accept more scholarships than what you need or you could be taxed on the excess. Another important tip to remember is to verify the legitimacy of scholarships by showing applications to your school counselor first.

MILITARY FAMILIES SHOULD LOOK FOR VETERAN'S AND VETERAN'S FAMILY BENEFITS

We all know about the existence of the GI Bill, but often states will offer additional educational benefits to children whose parents served in the military.

Amounts of aid, qualifications, and the availability of the program vary from state to state. The amount could be anywhere from a small monthly stipend to over $40,000 worth of tuition and fees. If either parent spent any active duty time in the armed forces, go to the website for your state's Department of Education or Department of Veterans Affairs for information.

For information on how individual schools administer the program, call the school you're interested in attending to speak to someone in the veterans affairs office. Most universities have a veterans affairs contact within the financial aid or admissions office. Most states require that the student attend a public school in the state where their parent enlisted. If a parent or child is a disabled veteran, contact the U.S. Department of Veterans Affairs as well.

Also, remember that there are scholarships available to active duty servicemembers, veterans, and their families. Look for scholarships that match any of your specific characteristics or talents.

Chapter Wrap-Up

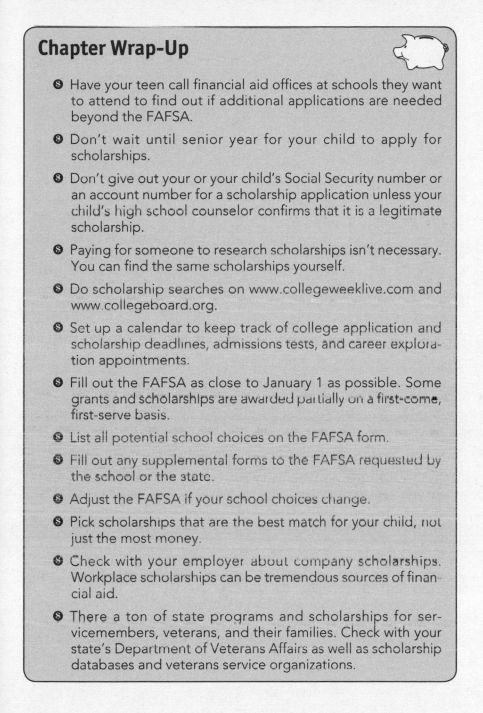

- Have your teen call financial aid offices at schools they want to attend to find out if additional applications are needed beyond the FAFSA.

- Don't wait until senior year for your child to apply for scholarships.

- Don't give out your or your child's Social Security number or an account number for a scholarship application unless your child's high school counselor confirms that it is a legitimate scholarship.

- Paying for someone to research scholarships isn't necessary. You can find the same scholarships yourself.

- Do scholarship searches on www.collegeweeklive.com and www.collegeboard.org.

- Set up a calendar to keep track of college application and scholarship deadlines, admissions tests, and career exploration appointments.

- Fill out the FAFSA as close to January 1 as possible. Some grants and scholarships are awarded partially on a first-come, first-serve basis.

- List all potential school choices on the FAFSA form.

- Fill out any supplemental forms to the FAFSA requested by the school or the state.

- Adjust the FAFSA if your school choices change.

- Pick scholarships that are the best match for your child, not just the most money.

- Check with your employer about company scholarships. Workplace scholarships can be tremendous sources of financial aid.

- There a ton of state programs and scholarships for servicemembers, veterans, and their families. Check with your state's Department of Veterans Affairs as well as scholarship databases and veterans service organizations.

8

Comparing Schools Through College Visits and Financial Aid Award Letters

This is probably the most important chapter in Section II. Why? Because selecting a college for the right reasons is vital to your child's success. I've had friends drop out of Harvard because it wasn't the right school for them.

In this chapter, I discuss what makes a school a "good school" for an individual student. Students shouldn't even think about this before doing the shadow days mentioned in chapter 6. After all, if they don't have an idea what they want to do, they may be disappointed that their major isn't available at the school they picked.

I talk about creating the list of schools in the "Senior Year" section of chapter 7, but students can begin to do this earlier in their high school career. After your child creates a list of the schools that might be a good fit for them as individuals based on all the information gathered in this section, it's time to compare financial aid award letters to determine which school works for them and is also a financial match. This brings me to our first topic in this chapter: the importance of college visits.

College Visits

College visits are important so your child doesn't pick a school simply because it's known as a "good school." During a college visit, they can go to the right departments and ask the right questions to determine whether it's a good school *for them*. While visiting, students can also stop by the financial aid office to see if there are other scholarships offered that aren't on the financial aid award letter. Armed with first-hand information, students can start the school application process with a foundation of schools to select from that match their criteria. After applying, they can compare financial award letters and offers.

WHAT YOUR TEEN SHOULD DO DURING CAMPUS VISITS

During campus visits, there are three primary tasks your teen should complete: visit the department office where their major is held, meet with someone about budgeting, and talk to career services.

Visit the department office: At the department office, your child can ask specific questions about what it's like to attend school there, such as:

- How much time will I spend studying?
- What kind of hands-on learning experiences and internships are available?
- Where are graduates from your department interning, and where are they working?

Your teen can also request a syllabus from first-semester courses. They may even have a chance to meet a professor or two. While in the department office, they should inquire about department specific scholarships, too.

Meet with someone about budgeting: Next, look for a place to talk about your budget. It's a growing trend for universities to have student money management offices staffed with peer counselors who can help you with budgeting from a perspective of a student who also wants to make sure they budget for club activities, food for late-night study sessions, going out with friends, and dating. Tuition, fees, room and board, and textbooks are important, too, of course.

How do you find the student money management office on your campus visit? University of Missouri Office for Financial Success Director Ryan Law suggests that before your visit, you search school websites for financial counseling, financial management office, and student money management. If nothing turns up, contact the school's financial aid office to see if it is aware of available resources on campus. Another potential resource is the on-campus credit union or bank. Ask what it offers year-round to help your child with budgeting and student loan repayment. Some schools offer video courses in student loan repayment.

Debunking Common Myths About College Budgets

Ryan Law, University of Missouri Office for Financial Success Director, debunks myths about college budgeting.

Myth: The cost of tuition covers the entire cost of going to college.

Fact: I'm a first-generation college student, and I thought this was the case when I went to college. However, there are a variety of expenses from textbooks to room and board that greatly impact your total spending.

Myth: If your child has a meal plan, you've accounted for the cost of *all* of their food.

Fact: Does your teen eat at the school cafeteria in high school? If not, they probably won't eat all of their meals at their campus dining hall. Students are so surprised at what it costs for fast food and entertainment. To reduce food costs, buy a meal plan that makes sense for them. If they'll eat one meal per day in the dining hall, buy the appropriate plan. I've seen families that bought a meal plan for two meals per day and then the student buys fast food for those meals. Thus, the family wastes over $300 per semester. Get your child a small refrigerator (dorm fridge) for their dorm room for easy and cheap breakfast foods such fruit, juice, and milk.

Myth: Students automatically get to live like adults at school.

Fact: There are student apartments with granite countertops, stainless-steel appliances, rooftop pools, and tanning beds. Ask yourself if it's worth the extra $1,000 or more annually in debt for these items. Students should compare all their housing options, with the safety of the neighborhood and proximity to campus as two of the most important considerations.

Myth: Your child can afford the debt they're offered.

Fact: Just because your child is offered a certain amount in student loans does not mean that they should accept it. They need to consider how much debt they have accumulated already, what the payment will be, and how this new debt will impact that payment. You can review current student loan debt at www.nslds.ed.gov/nslds_SA.

Myth: There's no way of predicting what entertainment and other miscellaneous expenses your student will have.

Fact: There are a number of places on campus you can call to talk with students who are currently on campus and have a good idea of what to plan for. You can find these resources in the student government office and student money management offices. The best part about your student making phone calls to find out this information is that you'll know if the schools they're considering have the support services available to help your child succeed financially.

What's nice about schools that offer budget counseling and resources is you know that your kids will be supported in that part of their education. My alma mater, the University of North Texas, has a great resource that offers a variety of workshops throughout the year on financial topics important to students.

Talk to career services: Before a student arrives on campus, they should set up an appointment with career services. This is a great time to discuss potential career paths within their major; the discussion may even influence jobs, internships, and shadow days during their final year of high school. The career center should be able to tell students what kind of internships to expect in different years and how the center will support them in career exploration in college.

I used to believe that pay rate post-graduation was important when researching careers and figuring out how much in student loans to borrow. However, you can make money in any field where you're good at what you do. I've been told over and over again that it's impossible to make a living as a freelance writer, yet I've done it for well over a dozen years and know many other freelancers who have as well.

Encourage your child to continue exploring different paths until they find the career they want with a reasonable amount of debt ($40,000 to $50,000 for an undergraduate degree), whether it's you or your child doing the borrowing. Just make sure they focus on proceeding academically as well. I changed majors as an undergrad, but in retrospect I would have been better off finishing up my degree and then getting a master's in journalism. I took the long way, but it still worked out.

Is there something your child absolutely loved about one school versus another? With the help of their school counselor, calculate the total student loan debt they could expect to borrow over the course of 4 years at all the colleges on your teen's final list. All schools in the top 5 list should be visited if possible.

With proper planning, your child should be able to find a college that's both affordable and helps them reach their goals.

TIPS FOR VIRTUAL VISITS

Your child can't personally visit each and every school before the list is narrowed down to five or so. Thus, virtual visits are incredibly important.

Here are a few things your child can do to visit a school online before deciding if they want to visit in person:

- Check both the school website and www.collegeweeklive.com for virtual campus tours. They also have live web chats with admissions officers. When looking at the virtual campuses, get a feel for what the campus is like. Does it have a lot of greenery? What are the facilities like?

- Call the student government office to find out about free activities on or near campus. Having an abundance of student activities can help reduce your budget and improve your child's social support system.

- Call the specific clubs they would like to be involved in, especially student professional organizations. These clubs may help your child get their first job.

- Make a phone appointment with other campus services such as the student money management office.

- Use the net price calculators on each school they are considering, but also talk to the financial aid office about potential scholarships and the likelihood of getting university grants.

Financial Aid Award Letters

When your teen gets a college acceptance letter, they should also receive a financial aid award letter. The financial aid award letter contains information on scholarships and other financial awards offered by the university, including federal loans and grants if available. Compare financial aid award letters to decide which school on your teen's list is the most affordable. They will want to be a good college consumer and compare career potential, too. Bring all the information you've gathered with you to the high school counselor meeting, including budgeting information, major, and college experience information.

If the schools' award letters are close, information contained in your notes may be the deciding factor.

Debunking Myths About Financial Aid Award Letters

Bob Bardwell, Director of School Counseling at Monson Innovation High School, debunks common myths about financial aid award letters.

Myth: It's all going to work out.

Fact: Too often I see students sign an award letter without understanding what's being offered. They think any money offered, loans or otherwise, is offered to them as free money or money they don't have to pay back. Since they haven't received a bill yet, they don't know what student loan payments will cost.

Myth: Deadlines to accept financial aid offers aren't important.

Fact: Deadlines are vital. Not signing an award letter on time can result in losing thousands of dollars. Too often, students don't sign documents on time and lose out on scholarship and grant awards.

Myth: There's no way of finding out if your school is affordable for you.

Fact: Net price calculators available on college and university websites will give you an estimate as to what kind of financial aid you might receive so you can best calculate actual cost.

Myth: I've put a child through college before so I know what I'm doing.

Fact: Families who have sent their older children to school might feel like they already know the process and what financial aid will be offered. Each school and each year is different. For instance, a school could have just received a new endowment or have one running out of funds, so they could have more or less endowment money each year.

Myth: Everything on the letter is financial aid.

Fact: There are categories such as *Help* that could refer to income the school expects the students to earn or contribute from their own savings and is often separate from work study. It is extremely important that students ask schools to clarify what a term on the award letter means in detail.

Myth: All award letters are the same.

Fact: Even the terms *grant* and *scholarship* can mean something different at each institution. A grant or scholarship could be need-based or merit-based, and each may or may not have guaranteed renewability based on grades, income, or other conditions. As a side note, a $15,000 scholarship to a school that costs $60,000 to attend is a wonderful gift, but it may not be enough of a reason for you to pick that school over a school where your family is given a $2,000 grant that has an annual cost of attendance of $20,000. With the $15,000 scholarship, you'd still be responsible for the remaining $45,000; but the $2,000 grant at the less expensive school means your financial responsibility would be $18,000 — that's a big difference.

Myth: It's cruel to tell your child they can't attend their dream school.

Fact: It's much crueler to have your family incur a $200,000 debt so your child can get an undergraduate degree. The answer may be that they attend their dream school after 2 years at a community college or after earning enough AP credits and summer credits at a community college to reduce their actual time at their dream school to just 2 years.

Myth: A student's college performance isn't influenced by whether or not they help pay for their education.

Fact: I've found that students do better in college if they have a personal stake in their education, such as hard-earned scholarships or a part-time job during or before college, where part of their earnings go toward college savings or current tuition costs.

Bottom line: Financial aid award letters are just pieces of paper. Make sure you understand what each term means and call the schools to clarify any part of the letter you're unsure about .

Caution

I can't emphasize enough how important it is to call schools for definitions of each and every award and part of the financial aid award letter.

Exercise: Building a Financial Aid Award Letter Chart

It's difficult to compare financial award letters that have different definitions for items on your list. Thus, it's important for you to create a chart that compares schools based on information you gathered. After calling schools and getting details on how they define items on your financial aid award letter, you'll be able to categorize everything and know the numbers behind each of the schools to which your child has been accepted. I've included an example of this chart here. There is also a basic version of this chart available for download in the resources section of graduationdebt.org.

Create one chart per school, and don't worry about subcategorizing grants or scholarships. It's also helpful to create a separate chart that just lists private scholarships such as community scholarships that your child wins, as these can be applied to different schools.

Financial Aid Award Letter Chart

Award Name	Money That Doesn't Have to Be Repaid	Conditions of the Award (If Renewable, Include Renewal Conditions)	Amount Reduced if Receives Private Scholarships?	Renewable?

Chart Categories

- **Award name:** This can be a grant, a scholarship, or even a student loan or work study.

- **Money that doesn't have to be repaid:** Scholarships and grants can both fit into this category. Answer this with a *yes* or *no*.

- **Conditions of the award:** Write down what the conditions are on each award. Student loans have a condition of a 2.0 GPA and minimum number of credits to receive more aid. Scholarships and grants can also fit into this category.

- **Amount reduced if receives private scholarships?:** Write a *yes* or *no* next to each award. To find out this information, ask the financial aid officer at the school to see if any scholarships or grants will be reduced if you receive private monies. You may not see any reduction, or it may just affect student loans.

- **Renewable?:** Is this money guaranteed to be renewed? Scholarships and grants may fit into this category. Note that student loans don't have guaranteed renewal.

If your child is applying to multiple schools, you may want to set up a Financial Aid Comparison chart like the one that follows to help you readily compare the opportunities at different schools.

Financial Aid Comparison Chart

	School 1	School 2	School 3	School 4	School 5
Money That Doesn't Have to Be Repaid (Add an X if Renewable)					
Student Money Offered from Work Study					
Parent Plus Loans					
Federal Student Loans					
Remaining Amount					

School Comparison Sheet

Have your child write out a quick list of the pros and cons of each school that sent them an acceptance letter. Then, as a family, discuss cost and what your child likes and dislikes about each school.

Comparing doesn't mean just picking the least expensive school. For instance, make one question part of the discussion: *Is the school you're considering better in training students for that major and career field than a less expensive school that you were accepted into?*

The bottom line is to pick a school that your child will enjoy and one that will help them along their career path without incurring a huge amount of debt.

In the next section I talk about financial decisions after the college choice is made. Good luck to your family on picking a college!

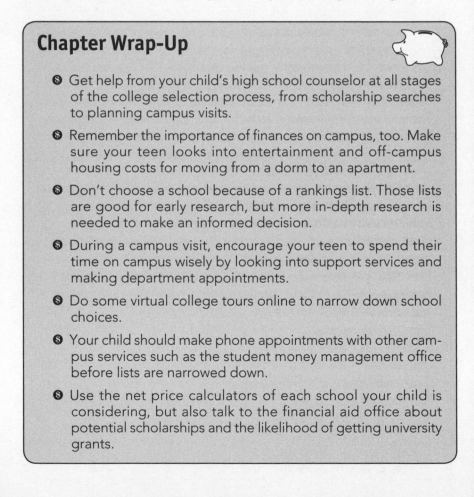

Chapter Wrap-Up

- Get help from your child's high school counselor at all stages of the college selection process, from scholarship searches to planning campus visits.

- Remember the importance of finances on campus, too. Make sure your teen looks into entertainment and off-campus housing costs for moving from a dorm to an apartment.

- Don't choose a school because of a rankings list. Those lists are good for early research, but more in-depth research is needed to make an informed decision.

- During a campus visit, encourage your teen to spend their time on campus wisely by looking into support services and making department appointments.

- Do some virtual college tours online to narrow down school choices.

- Your child should make phone appointments with other campus services such as the student money management office before lists are narrowed down.

- Use the net price calculators of each school your child is considering, but also talk to the financial aid office about potential scholarships and the likelihood of getting university grants.

- ⑤ Call the financial aid office of each school that sent your child a financial award letter to ask questions and clarify terms.
- ⑤ Create financial aid award charts for each school to note accurate numbers.
- ⑤ Create a separate awards chart for private and community scholarships.

Section III

Filling the Gaps:
For Parents of In-College Students

In this section, I talk about how to fill in the gaps left after scholarships, college savings, and grants. You'll learn about different types of loans as well as payment plans. If you have young children, you won't have to make these decisions for a long time. However, you will want to understand borrowing and payment plan terms well before these options are needed.

Borrowing Parent PLUS Loans

This chapter is the crux of why I wrote this book: I get nervous when parents put their financial futures behind that of their child. I've received more than one email from parents who wanted to cash in their 401K after a layoff to pay for their child's education or who were asking how they were going to pay for their child's *entire* education.

In the immediate future, federal parent PLUS loans seem like the way to go. They have built-in options for repayment and temporary payment breaks that private student loans may or may not have. They also have many of the same options as student loans, such as repaying loans over an extended period of time.

So what's the problem? There are a few, actually: Parent PLUS loans can be borrowed for excessively high amounts, income doesn't have to be proven, and interest rates are higher than those of student loans.

But that doesn't mean they don't have a purpose. It's possible the money borrowed will fill an affordability gap to help send your child to school.

In this chapter, I cover everything you need to know about federal parent PLUS loans, including limits, interest rates, approval requirements, and how to calculate how much you can afford to borrow.

Loan Limits and Interest Rates

Parents are allowed to borrow larger amounts than students. Traditional federal student loans have a reasonable annual and lifetime borrowing limit. A dependent student will be able to borrow $31,000 over their lifetime based on limits for the 2014–2015 school year. Annual limits vary from $5,500 to $7,500, depending on a student's year in school. Limits may change in the future.

However, parents can borrow up to the full cost of attendance minus any other aid.

For example:
A student's total cost of attendance is $30,000 for the year. The student's federal loans totaled $5,500, and they received $2,500 in scholarships. The parent can borrow $23,000. A parent could easily borrow over $100,000 over the course of attendance as tuition rates go up. But that doesn't mean you can afford $100,000. Income isn't a factor in approval, only credit history.

In addition to higher loan limits, interest rates for parents are generally higher than those for undergraduate students. Interest rates on parent PLUS loans are set annually on July 1 for the following year. The interest rate for parent PLUS loans for the 2015–2016 school year is 6.84 percent. The interest rate for undergraduate student loans is 4.29 percent—2.5 percent lower. Also, students with subsidized loans won't accrue interest while they're in school. Parent loans, however, will incur interest from the day you borrow each loan. So if you borrowed $25,000 in year one, 4 years later, you will have accumulated over $5,400 in interest on the first year's borrowing alone.

Interest rates can change every year, but they are always issued at a fixed rate. A fixed interest rate never changes, as opposed to a variable rate, which can change as the economy does. However, new loans will be issued at whatever the interest is for that year. For example, if interest rates for parent PLUS loans are set at 8 percent for the 2019–2020 school year, loans issued that year will always have an interest rate of 8 percent.

Loans can be repaid individually or averaged together if you choose to combine your loans via consolidation. I talk more about consolidation options in the repayment section (Section IV).

Before you get to repayment, you need to know how approval works and then calculate what you can afford to borrow. Your borrowing total should include private student loan borrowing, too. I discuss the combination of the two as well as borrowing strategies in the "Loan Chart and Loan Comparison" section near the end of chapter 10.

Applying and Getting Approved

Unlike traditional federal student loans, parent PLUS loans require a basic credit check and filling out a separate application in addition to the FAFSA. You don't have to accept all the loans you're offered, but applying is an important step in knowing your options once your child is already accepted and has received their financial aid award letter. The information here is also useful for parents of younger children because you'll learn about the credit requirements for approval.

To apply, go to the financial aid page of the university your teen will attend. Click on the parent PLUS loan application link and fill out the form. Proof of income isn't needed. You'll get a letter back stating that you've been denied or approved. The amount is always the full cost of attendance minus other aid. However, you can choose to borrow a smaller amount.

CREDIT REQUIREMENTS

The federal government doesn't require a parent to have pristine credit. In fact, they don't really care if you have any credit history. Only negative credit problems, such as those listed below, could prevent you from being approved for a parent PLUS loan:

- A bill on your credit report that is 90 or more days past due.
- A major negative credit event within the last 5 years (these derogatory events are defined in the federal regulations):
  - loan defaults
  - bankruptcy discharge
  - home foreclosure
  - repossessions such as of vehicles
  - county, state, or federal tax liens
  - wage garnishment, charge-off or write-off of federal student loans or grants
- An account charged-off or in collections with a non-zero balance.

What do you if you can't get approved for a parent PLUS loan? You have a few options:

- **Reapply later after catching up on an account such as a credit card or bank loan that's 90 days or more past due.** To make sure your accounts are current on your credit report, order a free credit report through www.annualcreditreport.com 30 days after catching up. If an account is not up to date on the reports, contact the company that holds the account and request that your information be updated.

- **Ask a relative or friend to endorse the loan.** Parent PLUS loans can have cosigners. Just remember, as far as the federal government is concerned, the cosigner is equally responsible for paying off the loan.

- **Look at other funding options.** Parent PLUS loans aren't your only option to fund your child's education, but you're unlikely to get a private student loan if you can't qualify for a parent PLUS loan. Think about payment plans or having your child look into a less expensive school for one or more years.

- **Appeal the decision if inaccurate.** You may have an error on your credit report that caused the denial. Review your credit report and dispute any inaccuracies. Then, wait 30 days before reapplying.

Debunking Myths About Parent PLUS Loans

Steve McCullough, President and CEO of Iowa Student Loan, which has a subsidiary company that services federal PLUS loans, provides the facts behind the misconceptions about parent PLUS loans.

Myth: A parent PLUS loan is a product of the federal government and therefore offers the same terms as other federal student loans.

Fact: Although parent PLUS loans are made through the Federal Direct Loan Program, administered by the U.S. Department of Education, they are unsubsidized loans for parents of undergraduates, or for graduate-level students as borrowers. Interest on a parent PLUS loan is charged during grace and deferment periods, and while the student is in school. Direct subsidized loans for undergraduates with financial need do not accrue interest while the student is in school or during grace and deferment periods.

Myth: Parent PLUS loan interest rates are the same every year.

Fact: The rate for a parent PLUS loan you take out this year can be lower or higher than a parent PLUS loan you received last year. You should always compare parent loan options from private lenders and the federal government each year to find the best option for you.

Myth: A parent PLUS loan is the only option when my student has exhausted all grants, scholarships, work study options, or federal student loans.

Fact: Private student loan options exist, though they often require a parent to serve as a cosigner. The student is the primary borrower, but responsibility to repay the debt falls to the cosigner should the student fail to do so.

Myth: Because the government knows my credit history and ability to repay, they'll only allow me to borrow what I need from parent PLUS loans.

Fact: A credit check will be performed during the application process, but a credit check is only a small piece of your financial ability to repay. A higher loan limit can lead to over-borrowing, leaving a heavy repayment burden on parents.

Myth: Parent PLUS loans offer the same federal safeguards as federal student loans.

Fact: Parents who borrow PLUS loans are generally not eligible for lower payments via income-driven options. However, they are eligible for income-contingent payments if they consolidate their loans into one direct loan. Since options can change in the future, always double-check this with the Department of Education when it comes time to consolidate.

Myth: My student can help me pay back the parent PLUS loan I took out for their education.

Fact: With parent PLUS loans, the parent (or a cosigner) is the only person legally obligated to pay back the debt. Should the parent experience financial hardship, responsibility to repay the parent PLUS loan does not fall to the student. The student will only help parents if they choose to do so.

Myth: Parent PLUS loans can be consolidated with the student's federal loans.

Fact: It's important to note that parent PLUS loans cannot be consolidated with any loans your student may have in their name.

> **Myth:** With parent PLUS loans, the government is more likely to work with me if I experience financial hardship.
>
> **Fact:** The federal government can and will exhaust all options to collect federal debts. This might include garnishment of Social Security and withholding income tax returns.

Calculating Approximate Monthly Payments

Let's imagine your child wants to go to a school that costs $30,000 per year and gets $10,000 per year in financial aid in the form of their own loans and scholarships. You consider paying the rest, but you only have enough available cash to pay the origination fee on the $20,000 you need to borrow and the interest while your student is in school. (The origination fee is the amount it costs to borrow the money before any interest accrues.) The origination fee on $20,000 is currently around 4 percent, which would be $800.

Note: Private student loans generally don't have origination fees but may or may not have differences in repayment terms. Private student loans are covered in detail in chapter 10, but we'll compare the two types of loans throughout Section III.

To determine what it would cost for you to borrow the funds via a parent PLUS loan, you can use the repayment estimator on the studentloans.gov website. For example, enter in $80,000 ($20,000 for each of the 4 years your child will attend college) with a 7.2 percent interest rate. The interest rate could go up or down, but let's use this number to estimate payments. Don't worry about entering income information because you want to see what you can afford without an income-driven option.

If the loan is paid off in 10 years (120 months), your payment would be over $900. An extended repayment plan for 25 years (300 months) would have a payment that's nearly $600. While the 25-year plan is tempting, are you prepared to still be making payments on student loans when you're 65 and beyond?

CAN YOU AFFORD THESE PAYMENTS?

If you're unsure what you'll need in 20 years, contact a financial professional such as your financial advisor or 401K manager to discuss how much you need for retirement. If they say you can't afford to make a payment that's more than $400 per month for 25 years or $600 for 10 years, then you should rethink how much you're borrowing. In this case, your advisor would probably say to keep your borrowing to about $50,000 maximum in order to reach these payment goals.

Even though you can't afford to borrow $80,000, that doesn't mean your child can't go to college. Look at other options, including financing, different schools, and your child taking some credits at a community college. The good news is your child may not have to change schools to take additional credits. I saved thousands by taking the prerequisites for my MBA program at a community college.

A private loan with a low interest rate could save you money, too. For instance, if you need $80,000 and can avoid paying origination fees, you can reduce borrowing by $3,200 ($800 × 4 years). Then, if the interest rate is fixed at 6 percent, your payment would be around $850 per month for 10 years or $500 a month for 25 years. Of course, the bank would have to offer this option.

Additional money for education can be generated if your student works part-time while in school. For example, your son or daughter may earn $5,000 or more per school year from part-time work. Of course, students should also look for last-minute scholarships which can be found in a variety of ways from online to the financial aid offices at the schools they're considering. Before picking a school, your child should contact career services to find out how much work co-op programs and internships pay in their area and career field.

Remember, if you can't afford to borrow as much as you'd like to help pay for your child's dream school, there are many other ways to pay for college. As a family, you may have to find a way to give your teen the future they want while still protecting your own.

Rules on Accepting a Parent PLUS Loan

The good news is not only do you never have to accept the full amount of a parent PLUS loan you are approved for, but you can also increase the amount later on in the year. For instance, let's say you're approved for $20,000 but you only need $10,000. However, the other $10,000 you expect not to need is based on your student's projected income from a part-time job. In the second semester, they cut back on their hours to focus on school. Now, you do need another $5,000.

According to Jim Brooks, Director of the Office of Student Financial Aid and Scholarships at the University of Oregon, you would just contact the financial aid office to make an adjustment. As long as your student completed their first semester of the year successfully, you're all set. Your student can follow the same process for federal student loans if they didn't borrow as much as they needed.

Why not just borrow the maximum you could possibly need? Since federal student loans have origination fees, you're automatically paying to borrow money the day you borrow it. Thus, even if you pay back the funds immediately, you just cost yourself an origination fee. The $5,000 extra borrowed in the example has an origination fee attached that's over $200.

Chapter Wrap-Up

- Parent PLUS loans are available up to the full cost of attendance minus any other form of financial aid.

- Parent PLUS loans involve a basic credit check but don't require income proof for affordability.

- Apply for a parent PLUS loan from the school's website.

- Interest rates are fixed and set once per year.

- Use the repayment estimator on the studentloans.gov website to calculate potential payments.

- You can borrow more later in the year if you didn't borrow the maximum allowed.

Everything You Need to Know About Private Student Loans

Private student loans are one of the most controversial and confusing types of loans. Yet they can have benefits, too, over the parent PLUS loans covered in chapter 9.

Why the confusion? Parents who have student loans under their name are used to federal student loan rules. Private student loans are bank loans and have their own rules determined by the lender for repayment plan and time frame options, as well as grace periods after graduation, dropping below a specified number of college credits, or not taking any credits in a semester.

Federal student loans also generally don't require a cosigner, so parents don't always understand that with private student loans, the parent is automatically equally responsible for the loan under their child's name.

Case in point: In 2013, there was a flurry of news stories about parents who were responsible for their children's student loan debt after their children died. If parents had fully understood their responsibility when they cosigned, they would have realized they were responsible for the loan if the student, for any reason, couldn't repay the debt, including if the student dies.

Since private loans are from private banks, the situation is similar to what would happen with a vehicle or home loan. When you cosign a car loan and the borrower can't make payments, you have two choices: The car gets repossessed (which negatively impacts your credit), or you agree to take over making the payments to save your credit.

What Is a Cosigner?

A cosigner is someone who legally vouches for the loan borrower that they will pay the loan if the borrower can't.

However, just like parent loans, private student loans do have their purpose in filling gaps left after federal student loans. They also can have lower interest rates, and they don't have origination fees.

In this chapter, I discuss everything you need to know about private student loans, including cosigner responsibilities. I also discuss creating a chart to compare all of your loan options, including parent PLUS loans, and how both private student loans and parent PLUS loans can affect you getting approved for other loans such as home and car loans.

Caution

While private loans approve an amount that is partially based on your income, that doesn't mean you should borrow that full amount.

Cosigner Release Agreements

One of the most important aspects of choosing a private student loan is selecting a cosigner release option. Always ask about this option as well as the terms for the release to be approved. A cosigner release means that after a certain number of on-time payments, normally between 12 and 24, the cosigner is no longer liable for the loan. Being released from the agreement helps both you and the student. Why?

For you, you no longer have to nag your child about making payments on time because the loan no longer affects your credit. Remember, the loan can also impact your ability to get approved for other loans. That's because you agree to pay the loan if your adult child doesn't. Your bank, other banks, and credit report agencies consider the loan yours, and therefore it is part of your credit record. So if you want to get a new mortgage, for example, the reported monthly payment amount will increase your debt-to-income ratio (the ratio of your debt payments to your income).

For your child, it's freedom in two ways: They don't need to discuss payments with you anymore. Plus, the loan servicer will no longer consider your income if your offspring calls in asking for a temporary payment break.

Before cosigning, make sure your college student knows that your credit is affected and to contact you before missing a payment. It's also important that your student borrows an amount they can afford to pay back. The career services department can help, as well as credit union financial counselors, and on-campus student money management and financial aid counselors.

You need to take your cosigner responsibility seriously and make sure that you can afford to pay back the loan if your child can't. When you discuss private student loans with your student, you should include how much you will chip in if they get into financial trouble, and how much if they don't. I recommend having a new conversation each year.

Understanding Variable Interest Rate Terms

In the past, all private student loans had variable interest rates. Now, you have options for fixed rate and variable rate loans. Before your family chooses a private student loan with a variable interest rate, you need to know the details, especially how and why your interest rate and payment can change.

Your interest rate terms are likely set based on the credit and the range the bank or lender offers. Notice I said *interest rate terms* instead of *an interest rate*. An interest rate is something you get with a fixed rate loan or a loan that is fixed for a period of time of a year or more.

For variable rate loans, your interest rate is based on an economic index, normally LIBOR or prime, which I tell you more about in a moment. The index acts as a basis for helping the bank figure out how much it will cost them to borrow the money they need to lend to you. "Banks just stand in the middle," says Dr. James Conover, finance professor at the University of North Texas.

Banks borrow the funds that they lend out, which changes in cost for the banks every night. How often your rate changes based on the index depends on your loan. You could have a loan based on a 1-month, 3-month, or 6-month index. However, your loan could be based on one of these indexes but change based on the terms the lender assigns in your contract. For example, a loan that is tied to the 1-month LIBOR index could change quarterly. This just means that your lender looks at the 1-month index every 3 months and assigns the indexed portion of your interest rate accordingly. With the indexes changing constantly due to the state of the economy and the overall loan market, the margin—the extra interest paid—on top of the index remains stable based on the borrower's or the cosigner's credit rating. This accounts for the risk to the bank of lending to you.

For example, you could have a rate of 1-month LIBOR plus 4 percent if you have a phenomenal credit rating. However, the same bank gives your buddy with not-quite-as-good-credit interest rate terms of 1-month LIBOR plus 10 percent.

LIBOR AND PRIME RATE INDEXES

As I've mentioned, the two indexes used as a basis for your student loans are LIBOR and prime. LIBOR (London Interbank Offered Rate) is the actual rate that many banks pay to borrow money on a short-term basis, such as when you see a 1-month or 3-month LIBOR rate.

When you look at the historic and current LIBOR index rates on the Federal Reserve website (www.federalreserve.gov), you'll notice the different lengths of time such as 1 month or 3 months. This is because a bank may borrow the money for loans for different time periods with the rate only being effective for that time period. So, if you have a rate that is linked to the 1-month LIBOR index, your rate could change for the bank every month. Let's look at an example of how your rate changes.

Say your interest rate terms are 1-month LIBOR plus a margin of 4 percent. The 1-month LIBOR rate could be 2 percent. Your interest rate for the term that your bank gives you this rate (your lender could set the interest rates to change every month, 3 months, or 6 months) would be 6 percent (4 percent plus 2 percent).

The next month, the 1-month LIBOR rate is 2.5 percent. If the terms of your loan allow for monthly rate adjustments, your interest rate for the month would be 6.5 percent (4 percent plus 2.5 percent). As you can see, the LIBOR-based portion of your interest rate changes, but your margin stays static.

Monthly prime rates work the same way. However, where prime and LIBOR differ is that prime is based on the absolute best rate lenders give their premium clients. The index is based on a survey of the prime rates from large banks. Because it is a rate given to premium clients instead of the rate the bank is actually paying, typically the prime index is a couple of percentage points higher than the LIBOR index.

CALCULATING POTENTIAL PAYMENT RANGES

In order to factor that your private student loan payment could be in your or your student's budget, you need to find a way to estimate what your future payments will be beyond at least the next reset period of 1, 3, or 6 months. Since your interest rate goes up and down, you can't just input a monthly payment into your bill pay and be done with it. But you can budget an amount based on the highest your loan rate could get. And when your rate doesn't reach the upper echelons of your interest rate range, you can use that extra money for other things, such as increasing your emergency fund or paying down your car loan.

There's only one problem with this plan: Unless you have a time machine handy to fly 15 to 30 years into the future to check out all the ups and down of the financial indexes for the life of the loan, you really won't know how high your interest rate will rise. However, you can look back at history to see how rates have varied in the past. The following table shows a sample period of 20 years from 1977 to 1997 for both LIBOR and prime.

Year	1-Month LIBOR Annualized	Prime
1977	5.75	6.83
1979	11.66	12.67
1981	16.72	18.87
1983	9.38	10.79
1985	8.12	9.93
1987	6.88	8.21
1989	9.16	10.87
1991	5.81	8.40
1993	3.07	6.00
1995	5.86	8.83
1997	5.52	8.44

Based on data from www.federalreserve.gov

As you can see, your interest rate can fluctuate quite a bit. But the most important part of this example is the increase in the indexes between 1979 and 1981: about 5 percent for LIBOR and about 6 percent for prime. This 2-year variance will help you determine an approximate interest rate range 2 years at time.

Add 5 percent to the interest rate you qualify for if you have a LIBOR-based loan, or add 6 percent to your current interest rate if you have a prime-based loan. Then use a simple loan calculator (such as those found at www.bankrate.com/calculators.aspx) to calculate what your payment would be with this potential higher interest rate. This will be the amount you factor into your monthly budget. You may never pay this amount, but you won't be caught off guard if it happens. Redo this calculation every year. Put a reminder on your calendar for your yearly student loan interest rate review. You can also ask your lender to do this calculation for you.

How Your Interest Rate Terms Can Change

Your rates can change based on such circumstances as missed payments on your private student loan, depending on the terms in your promissory note. Look for these terms and make a note on your loan chart (see page 101 later in this chapter). If you think you will have difficulty making the payments, contact your lender to discuss payment arrangements before it becomes a problem.

Note: You may decide to borrow both parent PLUS loans and private student loans. If this is the case, you should add them together to determine what you can afford to pay back.

Line of Credit

Another type of private student loan is a line of credit. Essentially, the difference between a line of credit and a loan is that one is for a specific amount and the other is an amount you can borrow. For instance, if you own a home and you decide to borrow against the amount you have already paid toward your mortgage, you can set an amount to borrow in a home equity loan or take out a home equity line of credit, where you're approved up to a specific amount but you have a choice of how much of it you borrow and when. Credit cards are another example of a line of credit.

The advantage to a line of credit is that families know the total amount awarded at the beginning of the student's college career, or after their first year applying. Thus, they can spread out the money as needed. For instance, a student may earn a scholarship in the first-year that they won't receive in their junior year or vice versa. A student may also pick up part-time work in some semesters and not others. Families should always discuss setting a limit on the line of credit.

As with other types of loans, repayment terms for a line of credit can vary. CU Student Choice works with credit unions to offer credit lines with a 6-month grace period for students enrolled at least half time and repayment periods of up to 25 years. They also offer graduated repayment plans.

Handling Private Student Loan Disputes

One of the scariest parts of borrowing from a private lender versus from the federal government is not having the same mechanisms in place to settle disputes—but that's changed in the last couple of years. Now, you can go online to the Consumer Financial Protection Bureau (www. consumerfinance.gov) to file a complaint in order to get help settling any dispute you have with your private student loan lender. It's also a good idea to research lenders before you borrow from them.

Loan Chart and Loan Comparison

In order to figure out what options you have for your private and parent PLUS loans, you need to look at all of them together in one file. The easiest way to do this is to create a chart. Remember to go through your credit report to find any loans you may have forgotten. For the rows, list all your private and parent PLUS loan options.

When you look at payments, consider all payments as your own in case your student is unable to make payments. To find out potential payments, have private lenders calculate payments or payment ranges for you. Add a row to your chart for a line of credit. A line of credit can also be a backup plan, but have the lender calculate the payment based on what you'd likely borrow. For instance, if you think you'll borrow $20,000 in private loans, put this in your chart with the payment for that amount. Remember, you can always borrow less than the full amount you're approved for on any loan.

You may decide to borrow a combination of parent PLUS and private loans. You may also borrow some money at a fixed rate and some at a variable rate.

Remember, all payments should add up to the amount your financial advisor says is your maximum to still reach your own financial goals. If your child does pay off the loans in their own name, which they probably will, you'll have that much more for retirement, but you should be prepared just in case. The bonus: By being frugal about the amount you borrow or cosign for, you're teaching your child to be frugal, too.

Even if you asked a financial professional to help you figure out a maximum borrowing limit, you should still seek advice on cosigner release options, the amount to borrow, and the amount to withdraw from your personal savings and investments. Loans, and paying for college as a whole, have a variety of moving parts. Double-check your decisions by reviewing your loan chart with your financial advisor, a credit counselor at a credit union, or another financial professional. These are long-term decisions that you want to evaluate as carefully as possible.

PRIVATE AND PLUS LOAN COMPARISON CHART CATEGORIES

- **Lender's name:** The name of the bank you're considering borrowing from.
- **Interest rate:** The interest rate for the loan.
- **Type of interest rate:** Fixed or variable.
- **Variable rate terms:** You'll want to write down the exact language that is used to describe your interest rate, such as *LIBOR plus 4 percent* or *prime plus 1 percent*.
- **Rules for interest rates increasing:** Ask for a sample promissory note and look for phrases such as the amount or if a missed payment can raise your rate. Anything like this should be included in your chart, along with the percentage by which your rate could change.
- **Cosigner release terms:** For parent PLUS loans, just put *No* because parent PLUS loans are solely your legal responsibility. For private loans, put the number of on-time payments and any other conditions.
- **Financial hardship rules:** Write down anything you see regarding forbearances or procedures for getting temporary payment reprieves or reductions in payments due to financial hardship.
- **Potential payments:** For variable rate loans, it's best to put a range. For all loans, you'll want to put a time frame with the payment, such as a 10-year payment option or a 25-year option.
- **Grace period length:** It's helpful for your student to have a time period before payments begin after graduation. Write down the information you're given.
- **Origination fees:** Generally, just parent PLUS loans have origination fees, but you should ask private lenders about this, too.

Private and PLUS Loan Comparison Chart

Lender's Name	Interest Rate	Type of Interest Rate	Variable Rate Terms	Rules for Interest Rates Increasing	Cosigner Release Terms	Financial Hardship Rules	Potential Payments	Grace Period Length	Origination Fees

Remember: You and your student have a variety of options to reduce debt burden. Review some of these options in chapters 11 and 12.

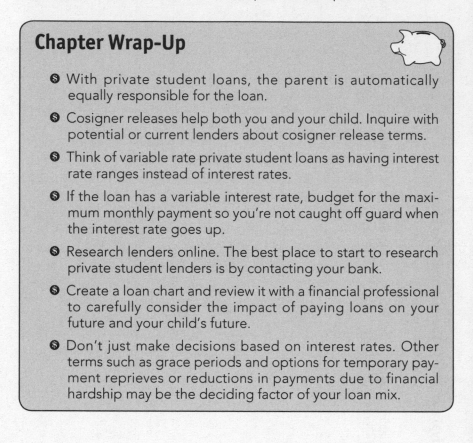

Chapter Wrap-Up

- ⑤ With private student loans, the parent is automatically equally responsible for the loan.

- ⑤ Cosigner releases help both you and your child. Inquire with potential or current lenders about cosigner release terms.

- ⑤ Think of variable rate private student loans as having interest rate ranges instead of interest rates.

- ⑤ If the loan has a variable interest rate, budget for the maximum monthly payment so you're not caught off guard when the interest rate goes up.

- ⑤ Research lenders online. The best place to start to research private student lenders is by contacting your bank.

- ⑤ Create a loan chart and review it with a financial professional to carefully consider the impact of paying loans on your future and your child's future.

- ⑤ Don't just make decisions based on interest rates. Other terms such as grace periods and options for temporary payment reprieves or reductions in payments due to financial hardship may be the deciding factor of your loan mix.

Finding Money to Chip in for Tuition During College

Parents who feel like they haven't saved enough for their child's college education don't have to stop contributing after the child is a certain age. In fact, when your child is in college may be the perfect time to contribute. You no longer have the living expenses you had from them living in your home, unless they are commuting to college. Also, you are probably making more than you did when your child was a preschooler.

However, not all monetary help you offer has to come out of your own bank account. Some may come from helping your child find cheaper and budgeted ways to attend college.

In this chapter, I discuss calculating how much you can afford to contribute from your funds, monetary gifts from relatives, and some budgeting tips. I continue the discussion in chapter 12.

At the end of this chapter, I include a handy chart to show you how to add up the free money. You know how I love charts.

Calculating How Much You Can Afford to Contribute

Let's start by thinking solely about the amount you can contribute from your budget on a monthly basis while your child is in college. We're not going to worry about specifics such as if you're going to give the money directly to the school, help out with living expenses, or deposit the money into a 529 plan just yet. This section is solely about what you can afford. I've divided the thought process into five steps:

1. **Decide if you're still going to claim your student on your tax returns.**

   If not, you'll want to deduct what you're getting back from taxes. For instance, if the tax year you're looking at has a $4,000 deduction per dependent and your tax bracket is 25 percent, you're getting back or reducing your payment by $1,000. More than likely you're still claiming your child. However, if you're not going to, you need to think about this amount in your budget difference.

2. **Think about whether your student will still live at home.**

   If they will, you won't be able to add the money you spent on their living costs to your college budget for them. However, you've already eliminated room and board costs.

   If your teen won't be living at home, you can factor in the amount you'll save by not paying their living expenses.

3. **Write down a list of the following expenses and see what you'll save or still pay.**

   If you're downsizing to a smaller home, there won't be any housing cost savings for families whose college-aged children aren't living at home.

   These are the usual expenses parents might save on:

   - **Groceries:** How much of your budget goes to feeding that one child? Include meals that your family eats out. This is an expense you won't save if your student lives at home.

   - **Clothing:** How much do you spend a year on clothing for your teen? If you're not sure, go through your bank or credit card statements in the past year.

   - **Allowances, sports, and lessons:** Account for money spent on allowances and extracurricular activities; these things can really add up. Also, think about other money you've given throughout the year for dating or going out with friends. Don't add birthday or holiday presents to this number, as you're likely not going to stop giving your student gifts.

   - **Car insurance and transportation:** If you've decided you're not going to have your student drive while attending school, you can deduct transportation expenses from your monthly budget. You may decide to leave them on your insurance while they're in school, but you won't be spending the same on gas as you were.

4. **Look at your budget as is.**

   Do you have extra money in your budget each month that you could redirect toward helping your child complete college? This doesn't mean you should get to the point where your budget exactly matches your paychecks. But if you have $500 per month in budget padding, you may want to redirect $250 of that amount toward college.

5. **Think about ways you can painlessly cut your budget.**

   I'm all about painless budget cuts. The bonus to cutting painless items from your budget is that you may find extra money for yourself, too.

   A painless budget cut is one that doesn't affect your lifestyle in the slightest way. For instance, if you compare home or auto insurance rates and get a better deal on the same coverage, you may save $1,000 per year. You could apply $500 of that savings to your student's college budget and get yourself a special treat with the other $500. Before changing insurance companies, always look at your state's Department of Insurance website to make sure potential new insurers have a good rating and don't have excessive complaints against them. If comparing rates online, use a comparison tool such as www.insurancequotes.com. You can also look for sites that are approved by the Better Business Bureau (BBB).

   You can find out if a website is a member of the BBB by looking for the BBBOnline logo. The BBB accepts and publishes information about the complaint history of thousands of companies. Enter the name of the website on which you are thinking about searching for car insurance prices into the search box at www.bbb.org to make sure the website has a good reputation. If you don't want to give out your personal information online, call a local independent insurance agent or company in your area.

   You also may be overpaying on your phone, cable, or electric bill. Ask your cable provider or telephone company about specials and bundling packages.

   Another painless cut is getting ridding of spoiled groceries. It's very common for families to throw out 25 percent of their grocery budget. If you spend $600 per month on groceries, that's $150 per month that's thrown away.

This is just a short list of how to save money. You'll find additional tips in chapter 1.

Total the savings and budget surpluses from following all these steps to figure out how much you can afford to contribute. Remember to think about your finances and future goals when determining the total amount you can afford to contribute to your child's college education.

Education Tax Benefits

One of the best ways to chip in for your college-aged child's education is with money given to you by the IRS or your state. Following are the most popular ways to get money back for your child's education:

The American Opportunity Tax Credit

This is absolutely my favorite credit and luckily, as of this printing, it was extended through December 2017. Families can get back up to $2,500 per child after filing their tax return. The first $2,000 spent on tuition and other qualified education expenses counts at 100 percent value. To get the next $500 back at a rate of 25 percent, you would need to spend another $2,000 on your child's education.

Don't use college savings or 529 plan dollars when calculating. That's considered double-dipping on your taxes and could cause you to lose the tax credit in the case of an audit.

Next, you need to know the income requirement. According to the IRS, "The full credit is available to individuals whose modified adjusted gross income is $80,000 or less, or $160,000 or less for married couples filing a joint return. The credit is phased out for taxpayers with incomes above these levels."

Note: All tax numbers aren't based on your annual salary. They're based on your modified adjusted gross income (MAGI) — your income after specific deductions. The easiest way to find your MAGI is by looking at your most recent tax return. You'll have a line on your form that has this number.

What does *phase-out* mean? In a specific income range, you'll get a reduced amount of the credit. For instance, with the American Opportunity Tax Credit, the current range for the phase-out is a MAGI between $80,000 and $89,999. For married couples filing jointly, the phase-out range is a MAGI between $160,001 and $179,999. How much of the credit you could potentially qualify for is based on how far into the phase-out you are.

For instance, a single filer who makes a MAGI of $85,000 per year is halfway through the phase-out and can potentially qualify for half the credit. The same goes for if you're married filing jointly and make $170,000.

File amended returns if you didn't declare your education tax credits in the last 3 years when you could have. There could be thousands waiting for you—a nice chunk of money you could put into your own 401K or use for your child's next year of education. Dependent students can claim the credit if parents don't. However, parents will probably see a larger refund since you can only get a refund of $1,000 if you didn't pay any taxes.

The American Opportunity Tax Credit works for the first 4 years for students studying at least half time. The Lifetime Learning Credit kicks in after that. If you go back to school, you should look into these credits for yourself, too. You can find more information on the IRS website (www.irs.gov). Also, if your income is too high to qualify for tax credits, you may qualify for other benefits such as tuition deductions. You can learn more about federal tax benefits by reading tax Publication 970 (Tax Benefits for Education) on www.irs.gov.

> ### Caution
>
> Tax information in this book is based on 2014–2015 tax rules. Remember, changes can happen in the future. Always check current tax credits and deductions with the IRS when your child is ready to attend college.

TUITION TAX CREDITS FROM YOUR STATE

Here's some really good news: You may be able to get tuition tax credits from your state as well.

For example, the state of New York offers tuition tax credits. If you are a resident of New York, you can get a state income tax credit that's a percentage of college tuition expenses of up to $10,000. For New Yorkers with allowable expenses of $5,000 or more, the credit equals 4 percent of allowed tuition expenses. For New Yorkers with expenses of less than $5,000, the credit equals the lesser of the applicable percentage of allowed tuition expenses or the applicable percentage of $200.

Thus, you could get another $400 for your student's education, depending on how much tuition you're paying for. States offer some other benefits, too, such as the tax benefits for depositing into a 529 plan (see chapter 2).

Some states even offer matching grants on your 529 plan contributions that are still available when your child is in college. For more information on when and how to get matching grants, see page 46.

Free Ways to Contribute to Your Child's Education

It doesn't seem to make sense, but you can actually contribute to your child's education without spending a dime. How is this possible? Through rewards from Upromise, credit card rewards, and family contributions. I talked in detail about all of these options in chapter 5, but family contributions to college savings for birthdays, holidays, or milestones don't have to stop after high school. You also shouldn't stop racking up your or your extended family's rebates from online shopping on Upromise. The main difference now is that you may want to change the way you receive Upromise rewards in order to avoid overfunding your 529 plan account.

Overfunding a 529 plan account, in my opinion, means putting in so much that you end up with a hefty tax penalty later: 10 percent of the withdrawal that's not used for your child's education, plus paying income tax on the part of the withdrawal that was from earnings.

CONTRIBUTING VIA FINANCIAL AND CAREER EDUCATION

Teaching your children about money is one of the best ways you can help them pay for college and really live better their whole lives.

Let's say you pay for your child's entire college education. They get out of school and haven't worked a job in their career field because you didn't talk to them about internships. Your child will have a harder time getting a job. According to a 2013 survey from the National Association of College Employers, students who had a paid internship while in school were twice as likely to get a job offer after graduation. Unpaid internships can also provide valuable experience and networking opportunities. Just have your student consult with career advisors to make sure the opportunities do help with overall career planning and confirmation of career and major choice.

WHAT ABOUT LESSONS ON MONEY ITSELF?

There are multiple ways for students to save money by budgeting well during college that will result in less student loan debt for everyone. A few of these are listed below:

- **Compare textbook options.** There a variety of ways to save money when it comes to textbooks — from buying and reselling smartly to renting textbooks when possible. I was able to get through both of my master's degrees by only spending $500 total on books. I could have easily spent $2,000. I saved $1,500 by reselling books on Amazon when my school bookstore didn't offer me enough. Although my school was no longer using the older edition of a textbook, other schools somewhere in the country were.

  I also bought a lot of books online, but I always double-checked with my professors first as to the edition that was needed as well as if CDs or digital codes were used for the course. If so, I also double-checked with the textbook seller to make sure these were included.

  Sometimes students will only have a choice of a digital book or prepared materials from the professor combined with a publisher's materials. These items normally can't be found cheaper.

- **Teach them about the real price of items.** An accounting professor in my MBA program taught me one of the most important lessons I've ever learned: If a store offers a 40 percent sale all the time, it's not a sale. You're paying a markup when you buy an item in that store that's not "on sale." I Google for promo codes before shopping trips. I've called stores ahead of time to negotiate with them about offering their online sales in-store. For electronics, Microsoft offers special student pricing, and Best Buy will match Amazon prices. Every time I shop at Best Buy, I enter the item description into my smart phone to see if I can find a cheaper price that they'll match.

- **Have them review their budgets monthly.** Your student should use free online tools such as those offered by www.mint.com to review their spending. Mint.com allows users to gather their credit cards and other account information on one secure site. They can then view their overall spending in one place. When I used mint.com the first time, I was shocked by how much I spent on dining; I made changes to reduce costs.

- **Teach them to talk about money with their peers.** By talking to their peers about their spending, they may be able to learn some new money-saving tips. Also, they can talk to career services and their professors about what is standard pay at internships and part-time jobs. This openness about salaries will let them know when they're being underpaid and potentially prompt them to ask for more money or to look for a better job. Of course, before doing this they should also talk to career services or one of their professors to find out why that may be the case and construct a good course of action. In addition to these on-campus resources, I'm a big proponent of student money management offices with peer counselors and credit unions that offer financial counselors.

- **Ask them to prioritize their own personal must-haves.** Learning what's important to them in their budget will help them make smart money decisions their whole lives. For instance, I will never give up coffees out, but I can give up expensive dinners or designer shoes without blinking. Your student needs to be able to prioritize what's important to them and what they'll do to pay for it. For instance, if a spring break trip is in the works, they need to think about whether that money will come from a part-time job or a student loan refund check. If it's from a student loan refund check, they need to think about the interest they'll pay for up to 30 years for one vacation.

Teaching your student these basic tips will save them money for the rest of their lives.

Adding It Up

Now it's time to add up this free money to see how it can help you further contribute to your child's education costs. Take a look at the following sample chart.

Your Available Contributions (Recalculate Annually)	
Source	Amount Gathered
Upromise rewards from yourself and family members	
Tax credits	
Budget surplus already available	
Personal budget savings from cutting items you're not enjoying (monthly, so ×12)	
Budget savings versus when your child was living under your roof	
Total	

Chapter Wrap-Up

- ⑤ Review your own budget for painless ways to make cuts.
- ⑤ Calculate differences in expenses from when your child is in high school versus in college, and then determine how much of this savings you want to put toward their education.
- ⑤ With the American Opportunity Tax Credit, families can get back up to $2,500 per child after filing their tax return.
- ⑤ Calculate your tax deduction and credit possibilities for both the federal government and your state.
- ⑤ Check tax rules at least once per year for new or updated education benefits.
- ⑤ Family contributions to college savings for birthdays, holidays, or milestones don't have to stop after high school
- ⑤ Discuss career services, internships, and budgeting with your child.

Changing Your Strategy During College

For a variety of reasons, your strategy for paying for college may have to change once your child is in college. It may be due to a change in college choice or a change in the income you thought you'd have when the child was born. Your child may also decide to go to grad school, and then you may decide to stretch your college savings for a few more years. Whatever the reason, the most important thing to do is to think about where you are now.

In this chapter, I cover filing renewal FAFSAs, applying for special circumstances benefits if your income drops, setting up payment plans, doing an annual assessment of your strategy and of where you are in regard to future years of college, and transferring schools when needed.

Fill Out Renewal FAFSAs Carefully

As I discuss in previous chapters, filling out the FAFSA is one of the most important things you can do to secure financial aid, including scholarships and grants from the school. Renewal FAFSAs, the forms filled out for the second year of college and beyond, are just as vital as the initial one. Forgetting to fill out a renewal FAFSA can cost your family thousands.

I've included another of my most popular forbes.com articles in this chapter because it busts a lot of myths about the FAFSA. Even if your child is in their junior year of college, I encourage you to read my other forbes.com article, reprinted in chapter 7.

Five Surprising Facts About Renewal FAFSAs

When you're filling out the Free Application for Federal Student Aid (FAFSA) for the second year or beyond, there may be some surprises. The term used for the annual form you fill out to apply for financial aid after your first year is *renewal FAFSA*. While the process of filling out the form is pretty much the same as when you filled out the initial FAFSA, you'll notice some differences.

Martha Holler, Sallie Mae spokesperson, provides a few tips for families to avoid being caught off guard by a few of the biggest surprises seen when submitting a renewal FAFSA.

1. Deadlines haven't changed.
Whether you're filling out the FAFSA for the first time or the 80th time, the school and state deadlines haven't changed. This is why families shouldn't wait to fill out the FAFSA until the 15th to 22nd of January, when reminders are sent out from the Department of Education. While some priority deadlines for school and state financial aid won't occur until after February 1st, some will occur earlier. According to Holler, Alaska, Vermont, and Washington request that students fill out the FAFSA as close to January 1st as possible. State and university need-based aid may be awarded on a first-come, first-serve basis.

2. Your school choice isn't autopopulated.
Some information is saved from previous years, but your school selection information isn't. Is this a bad thing? Not at all. If it was autopopulated and you transferred to a new college or university, or will transfer before next year, you could miss out on financial aid from your new school because of missing the deadline. If you're not sure if you'll transfer, put your current school and potential school on the list.

3. Cost of attendance could change.
The student may have lived in a dorm the first year and will now live off campus. Knowing the cost of the apartment isn't necessary, but stating *off campus* as the housing option is. Why? The cost of attendance could change, and thus, so could your total aid awarded.

4. You have to fill out a renewal FAFSA every year.
It's common to think that once you've filled out the FAFSA, you're done. Not so. Every year, families need to restate what their current income is because it fluctuates. In some cases, this means more aid. In some cases, a

change in income means less aid. If family income has already dropped for the year because of a circumstance such as for a job loss, submit a Special Circumstances form to your school. Talk to the financial aid office to get a copy.

In order to fill out a renewal FAFSA, all you need is your name, birth date, Social Security number, and PIN (personal identification number). Your PIN is the access number created on your first application. Parents who are helping their students fill out the application should remember each of their college-aged children will have a different PIN.

5. Tax information may have to be changed.
If you haven't filed a tax return, you can input last year's tax information and then change it when your income taxes are filed. You can also estimate income, but you have to know quite a bit of tax information to do it. Thus, you might as well use the previous tax year's information as a place holder.

Final thought: Filling out the FAFSA is one of the smartest things you can do to get money for your or your child's education. If you forget to fill it out or fill it out late, you could possibly lose out on thousands of dollars of financial aid.

This article originally appeared on forbes.com.

Fill Out the Special Circumstances Form If Income Drops

Have you always wondered what the silver lining is if a drop in income occurs? Potentially more financial aid, including grants and scholarships, for your college-aged student. Following are answers to some questions you may have about applying for special circumstances benefits:

How does your family apply for additional financial aid due to an income drop? The college student needs to pick up a Special Circumstances form. Your student can also request the form from the school they will attend next year, as the school already has their FAFSA information.

What if you never filled out a FAFSA? You can submit one now online using last year's tax return information and then submit the Special Circumstances form to communicate your current income.

Why do you submit the Special Circumstances form to the school instead of to the U.S. Department of Education, which administers the FAFSA form? While the government calculates the Expected Family contribution with the numbers you submitted, the school decides what the information will mean in regard to your student's financial aid package.

Whose income matters on the Special Circumstances form? Your student should fill out the Special Circumstances form if they, or you, have a drop in income—for example, if they will decrease their work hours this year due to a heavier course load.

Note: The other bonus to an income drop is you may qualify for education tax credits you didn't qualify for previously. Review Publication 970 (Tax Benefits for Education) and your state's treasury department's website.

After you've submitted the form, have your student ask the school what new scholarships or grants they might receive and the time frame for the decision. You may know in as little as a few weeks if you're going to get hundreds to thousands of dollars in additional financial aid for your child.

Payment Plans

Remember in the last chapter, when you calculated how much you could afford to contribute while your student is in school? If you didn't do that yet, go back and do it now.

Now that you have that number, one way to make the best use of the money that you're contributing while your student is in school is by signing up for a payment plan. A payment plan is normally offered by the school accounting office, so you can pay for tuition and fees and potentially on-campus room and board over the course of a semester. This helps families reduce their student loan borrowing if they'll have the money relatively soon.

There are fees attached, but they are generally cheaper than the 4+ percent origination fee attached to parent PLUS loans. And you don't have to put the full amount owed on a payment plan.

For instance, let's say your student's total account balance is $10,000 after all other forms of financial aid are applied to your student's loans. You received a $2,500 tax refund because of the American Opportunity Tax Credit from last year, so you decide to put the remaining $7,500 on a payment plan. If the fee is 1 percent of the amount you're paying off, you saved $25 versus borrowing the full $10,000. If you had borrowed a parent PLUS loan instead for $7,500, you would have spent around $250 more to borrow a loan for the same time period. That's why parent PLUS loans should be used if you won't have the money for a longer period of time. This is just one example of why you need to compare options to find the proper balance of savings strategies. If your student is working part-time, they may also want to take advantage of a payment plan to avoid their own student loan debt.

Learn more about payment plans in the "Debunking Myths About Choosing Payment Plans" sidebar that follows.

Debunking Myths About Choosing Payment Plans

Jim Brooks, Financial Aid Advisor for the University of Oregon, covers the myths and facts about payment plans.

Myth: All schools offer payment plans.

Fact: The choice to offer payment plans is up to each institution. If the availability of a payment plan is something that will impact your ability to attend the institution, you should find out available payment options before deciding where you will enroll. Information on payment options should be available on the institution's website.

Myth: All schools that offer payment plans have similar time frames for repayment.

Fact: Payment plans can differ across institutions. They may be spread out over one term, or the whole school year. Do your research so that you are prepared.

Myth: Payment plans are always called *payment plans*.

Fact: An institution may call payment options by different names. If you can't determine what the institution calls their payment plans, call the office responsible for collecting payments. They can provide that information. Examples of names include *tuition payment plan, deferred tuition payment plan,* and *tuition deferral plan*.

Myth: Payment plans are free.

Fact: Many institutions charge a fee in order to use their payment plan. That fee could be a flat dollar amount or a percentage of your outstanding balance after each payment or a finance fee. Be sure you find out this information early on in the process so you are prepared.

Myth: All payment plans are advertised.

Fact: Institutions exist to serve students and will typically try as hard as they can to assist students. While an institution may not advertise a payment plan, in some circumstances, institutions will make special arrangements with students who encounter problems making payments. If you find yourself in this type of situation, you should contact the institution to see what options are available.

Myth: You can't get on a payment plan while waiting for financial aid to arrive.

Fact: Institutions recognize that there are times when a student's financial aid may be delayed for one reason or another. Typically, if the reason is the student's fault (for example, they didn't apply for aid on time or they failed to complete requirements or submit documentation), the institution may be less likely to make exceptions. However, if the delay is due to a special circumstance or the institution inadvertently caused the delay, they might be willing to work with you to ensure that you are not penalized by the delay in your financial aid. Be sure to talk to your financial aid administrator in these types of situations to see if they can assist you.

Take an Annual Assessment

Every year, families should take a look at how much their college savings are, what money they'll have available, and what the school is offering their child in terms of financial aid. It's very important for the student to be a part of this exercise, even if it's by phone or video chat. Here are the steps you should take for your annual assessment.

1. **Review financial aid award letters annually.** Every year, your student gets a new financial aid letter with new offers for scholarships, grants, loans, etc. (If need be, go back to pages 73–78 in chapter 8 and review how to decipher financial aid award letters.) The key is to recategorize the information in the award letter into

Date due: 7/23/2016,23:59
Item ID: 31488006509657
Title: Parents' guide to
paying for college and
repaying
Author: Gobel, Reyna, 1977-

Date charged: 7/2/2016,14:
19

RENEWAL
DATE_____
RENEW ONLINE WITH YOUR
CARD AT
www.parkridgelibrary.org
OR CALL 847-590-8706

terms and descriptions you'll actually use, such as *scholarship is renewable for 4 years provided minimum GPA is maintained*. Use a chart like the one on page 77 in chapter 8 to fill in the information offered. Then fill in the Annual Paying for College chart (see the sample chart at the end of this list) with the resources your family actually uses. A nifty item you can add in the second year onward is the tax credits you received from tuition paid for in year one. Remember, your child can generally claim tax credits that you didn't, even if your child didn't work. The main reason to have your child take the credit is if your income was too high for you to qualify.

2. **Plan remaining college savings distributions.** Look at how much you have left of savings allocated for your child's college education. Then think about how much longer your child will be in school. You may decide to divide it evenly among all their remaining years. Each year, you can change how you allocate remaining savings.

3. **Decide how much you are you comfortably able to contribute.** Look back at chapter 11 to calculate the annual or monthly amount you can contribute to your child's education.

4. **Have your child apply for additional scholarships.** Luckily, those who become more academically focused in college than they were in high school may qualify for more academic scholarships. Make sure your student checks with the financial aid department and their academic department. Private scholarships and scholarships based on other student talents and activities may also be available. Take a look the collegeweeklive.com scholarship database each year.

5. **Calculate loan payments for both you and your child on a semester-by-semester basis.** You don't want you or your student to have a shock after graduation of a $1,000 payment no one was expecting. The servicers for the loans you borrow will be happy to calculate the loan payments for you.

   If payments are too high, this is a great time to think about changing up the loan mix for the next semester, such as how much is borrowed privately or via parent PLUS loan options. The student should exhaust their traditional federal student loan options before considering private loans or parent PLUS loans.

6. **The student should do a career experience assessment at career services.** This way you can ensure that your student is

taking part in career exploration exercises such as shadow days and internships.

7. **Talk to your student about their monetary contributions from part-time work or internships.** Another great reason for them to visit career services!

Note: Don't have your child pick careers based solely on which professions are high earning or are in high demand. Talent, ambition, and planning go a long way toward making any career choice an option. I've seen massive layoffs of journalists, but I've been a happy freelance writer since I was 19!

Here is an example of the categories you should include on your Annual Paying for College chart:

Annual Paying for College Chart	
Source	*Amount Expected This Year*
Scholarships	
Grants	
Student money offered from working	
Private student loans	
Money from 529 plan	
Federal student loans	
Parent PLUS loans	
Money budgeted for installment plan	
Money paid on tuition due dates	
Money from family and other sources	
Total	

Transferring Schools When Needed

It's a hard decision for families to make, but sometimes it's best financially and/or education-wise for a student to transfer schools. I transferred as a senior. When I originally went to college, I wasn't ready. I took some time off and then went back and completed two master's degrees after completing my undergraduate degree.

The decision to transfer shouldn't be taken lightly, and it's not always a wise idea. The main concern for me, and for most students who transfer, was whether the difference in course requirements would cause me to graduate later. I was able to thwart most of the financial differences.

If I had depended on just the courses that admissions would have accepted, I would have had at least 12 less credits. However, I got syllabuses from former professors to show my coursework was the same as a differently titled course at the new school. I also submitted a portfolio to get excused from an upper-level course that the other university taught at a lower division level. In addition, I took a few courses at the local community college to save money.

The new school also had a better journalism program suited to the conversational style in which I like to write. I called two other state schools and asked them about their journalism program—where their students were interning, where their graduates were working, and why I should choose their school over my other options. The department advisors in the school I ended up choosing gave me the best answers. No amount of online research could have replaced the hour I spent on the phone.

Finally, I transferred because I had moved to a different state and needed to pick a new in-state college if I ever wanted to graduate. I don't regret my decision in any way. I stayed at the new university to complete both of my advanced degrees.

Use the following chart to compare some of the financial pieces involved in a transfer:

	School 1	School 2
Additional credits required		
Cost of credits		
Any financial aid differences		
Cost of living differences		

Your family shouldn't base their decision on transferring solely on financial reasons, but finances should be part of your student's overall plan. You should discuss with them why they want to transfer and how transferring schools will benefit their long-term success.

If financial need is the reason for the transfer, consider a summer at a community college to reduce total expenses. I've heard of students being able to afford to attend elite schools that offer very few scholarships because they attended community college for the first 2 years.

Also, if the transfer is due to an income drop by you or your student, make sure a Special Circumstances form was filled out first to see if your student might qualify for more financial aid and be able to stay at their current school.

Learn more about transferring in the "Debunking Myths About Transferring Schools" sidebar that follows.

Debunking Myths About Transferring Schools

Craig Munier, Director of Financial Aid at the University of Nebraska–Lincoln, debunks common myths about transferring schools.

Myth: Transferring is solely about affordability.

Fact: In my experience, transferring is rarely about affordability, with the exception of students who may have crossed state boundaries and found the school impossible to afford due to having to pay nonresident tuition. Transferring is about a change of academic direction to something your current school doesn't offer, relationships either begun or ended, being closer to or farther away from family, and other factors.

Myth: It's always best to transfer to a less expensive school.

Fact: Cost should rarely be the first or only consideration. Fit, curriculum, and opportunities for success are more important. Once you are deciding on schools for the right reasons, then you can begin to explore affordability, financing, cost-to-value comparisons, and other considerations.

Myth: Transcripts alone are enough to receive the same credits at another school.

Fact: Credit almost always "transfers"; the question is whether it will meet degree requirements and adequately cover basic content to support more advanced courses on the subject. For example, it's one thing to transfer an English composition class if you are majoring in music; it's something entirely different if you plan to be an English major.

Myth: The next school will have exactly the same programs.

Fact: Many curriculums are offered at most schools. Some schools intentionally create "designer" curriculums intended to lead students to believe "they have the only such program in the country." This is rare, and such programs are usually so narrowly focused that they actually narrow graduates' options for employment.

Myth: No research is needed before transferring.

Fact: Transferring is not something to be taken lightly. Because of how credit may or may not meet degree requirements, simply transferring schools can lead to a semester, a year, or more of additional time in college solely because transfer credit doesn't meet degree requirements at the new school. Do your research so you don't waste valuable time or money.

Chapter Wrap-Up

- You will need to complete a FAFSA form for every year that your child is in college. Plan to fill out the FAFSA as close to the January 1 date as possible.

- If your income or your student's income drops, submit a Special Circumstances form to see if your student qualifies for additional financial aid.

- You can fill out a Special Circumstances form even if your child hasn't attended classes yet so that need-based aid award offers can be updated.

- You don't have to put the full amount you owe on a payment plan.

- Balance borrowing with payment plans when you can afford to do so.

- Talk to the financial aid office before choosing a payment plan.

- Review financial information on an annual basis, as some information may have changed.

- Start your annual assessment by recategorizing information on the financial aid award letter into usable information.

- Each semester, recalculate loan payments based on total borrowing up to that point. Enlist the help of student loan servicers in calculating post-graduation repayments.

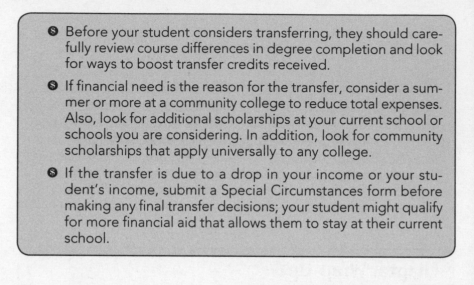

- Before your student considers transferring, they should carefully review course differences in degree completion and look for ways to boost transfer credits received.

- If financial need is the reason for the transfer, consider a summer or more at a community college to reduce total expenses. Also, look for additional scholarships at your current school or schools you are considering. In addition, look for community scholarships that apply universally to any college.

- If the transfer is due to a drop in your income or your student's income, submit a Special Circumstances form before making any final transfer decisions; your student might qualify for more financial aid that allows them to stay at their current school.

Repaying Federal and Private Student Loans:
For Parents of College Grads

- Chapter 13: Repaying Federal Student Loans, Including Your Own
- Chapter 14: Repaying Private Student Loans
- Chapter 15: Looking to the Future: Saving or Planning for Continuing Education

This section is mainly for parents who have borrowed student loans for themselves or for their children. This is a great section for parents of younger children and those with kids in college now to skim because it gives them an idea of what to expect. Chapter 15, the final chapter, is for families considering graduate school for their children or for themselves. Chapter 15 is primarily for parents of older students, but it's a good chapter for those with children who are planning to go to grad school.

Repaying Federal Student Loans, Including Your Own

If you have student loans of your own from your education, that repayment can last well into funding your child's education. In this chapter, I talk about repayment options for federal student loans for parents who borrowed for themselves or for their child. I also cover helping your student pay off loans they borrowed under their own name.

IMPORTANT NOTE: Throughout this chapter, when I refer to "your loans," I mean loans from your own education that you may still be repaying, as well as loans you've taken out for your child's education.

Gathering Information on Your Federal Student Loans

Before you can decide whether you want to consolidate your loans or choose a different repayment plan, you need to gather all the information you can on the loans that you have. The good news is that this is an easy process.

Log on to the National Student Loan Data System (NSLDS) at www. nslds.ed.gov, the federal government website that contains information on all of your federal loans, including what servicers you are with, how much you owe, and the status of your loan. Then, with the servicers' contact information, you'll make phone calls to find out payment and interest rate information that you'll compile in the chart exercise later in this chapter (see page 133).

To gather your federal student loan information, take the following steps:

STEP 1: REPLACE YOUR PIN

When you applied for your federal student loans of any kind in the past, including parent PLUS loans, you received a PIN (personal identification number) to access your federal student loan information.

The PIN system was replaced in the spring of 2015 with a username and password system. This is similar to what you probably have with your bank account. If your PIN is active (used or created relatively recently), you'll go through a simple process of creating a username and password when trying to access federal government sites that are used to apply for or that contain your federal student loan information. The username must be between 6 and 30 characters long and include any combination of numbers and/or letters. The password must contain three of the following: numbers, uppercase letters, lowercase letters, and special characters. If your PIN wasn't active or you don't have one at all, you'll have to answer challenge questions and provide information such as your Social Security number and date of birth when creating your username and password.

STEP 2: ACCESS THE NATIONAL STUDENT LOAN DATA SYSTEM

Now that you have your username and password, sign in to the NSLDS at www.nslds.ed.gov. Brace yourself because you are going to see how much interest has accrued since the first day you borrowed your first student loan dollar. If you've made payments on your loans, the amounts won't be as high. For your parent PLUS loans, you could have easily accrued several hundred to over a thousand dollars annually in interest, especially if you borrowed $10,000 or more.

On the NSLDS home page, click on Financial Aid Review. Accept the terms and enter your Social Security number, the first two letters of your last name during college, your date of birth, and your password. The first page you will see is a chart displaying a list of your loans with the following information: type of loan, loan amount, loan date, disbursed amount, canceled amount, outstanding principal, and outstanding interest. What do all these terms mean, and how is this chart going to help you manage your loans? Your NSLDS loan chart will give you all the information you need to find your student loans and information about them. However, if the chart just looks like a bunch of gibberish with the dozens of terms you need to know, you won't get much out of it. So in Step 3, I explain the terms that will be most important in deciphering the information you need.

STEP 3: REVIEW TERMS FOR TYPES OF LOANS

The federal government categorizes your loans in several different ways:

Consolidated: This is a combined loan from multiple semesters. For example, a consolidated loan from an undergraduate degree could have eight semesters' worth of loans consolidated into one.

Subsidized: With a subsidized loan, the government pays your interest while you attend college and other special circumstances.

Unsubsidized: With an unsubsidized loan, you pay your own interest in all circumstances.

FFEL (Federal Family Education Loan) Program: These loans are with a servicer other than the government, but they are federally backed loans and qualify for most of the same repayment programs as direct loans. They can also be consolidated to direct lending.

Direct: This kind of loan is issued directly from the government via direct lending as a servicer. Post June 2010, all federal loans issued are direct loans.

Stafford: The Stafford loan is the most common type of federal loan. It can come in many forms, such as consolidated or unconsolidated or subsidized or unsubsidized. It can be serviced by either direct lending or another servicer.

Note: The Stafford program was essentially replaced with a direct loan label. There really is no difference in how your loans are repaid. However, the direct loan label makes a difference in consolidation and Public Service Loan Forgiveness options. I go into this a bit more later in this chapter.

Caution

If you consolidated your loans after graduation, it doesn't mean all of your loans were consolidated. If you forget to name a loan to your servicer, it may have fallen by the wayside. When you construct your Personal Student Loan chart later in this chapter (page 133), look at the balances owed on all your loans, whether or not you believe a balance was consolidated.

Perkins: A Perkins student loan is a need-based loan and is normally reserved for low-income families. If you have a Perkins loan, you may have additional options for loan forgiveness.

Loan Amount: This is the amount you were approved to borrow for a specific semester. This amount may not have been the amount you received. For instance, let's say you were approved for $6,000, but you decided you only needed $3,500. You don't have to pay back the other $2,500 you were approved for because you never borrowed this money.

Loan Date: This is the date you originally took out your loan. It is helpful in deciphering in which semester you borrowed that particular amount of money. Be aware that you could have more than one loan per semester. For example, let's say the government gave you x amount of money in a certain semester in a subsidized loan where your interest is paid while you attend college. Then you were given an additional loan to cover the rest of your expenses in the form of an unsubsidized loan. You had two loans total for that one semester.

Disbursed Amount: This is the original amount of money you borrowed on the specified loan date. It has nothing to do with how much you owe now, because interest has accrued and payments may have been made. You can pretty much ignore this category unless you never actually borrowed the money and need to dispute the charge, similar to a mistake on your credit report. I talk about what to do with an inaccurate listing later in the chapter (page 135).

Canceled Amount: If you see a canceled amount, it means that amount is no longer owed. It could be canceled for a variety of reasons: Perhaps you became disabled and could no longer make payments because you could not work, you completed a loan forgiveness program, or you rejected part of the financial aid package you were rewarded. For example, I applied for financial aid in my last semester of school. However, I looked at the debt I'd already accumulated and decided I didn't want to accrue more student loan debt. So I arranged a payment plan with my university to pay over the course of the semester instead of taking on new debt. For that particular semester, a cancelled amount is shown on my loan chart for the loans I turned down.

Outstanding Principal: This is the amount of your original loan that you still owe. However, outstanding interest is added to this amount to create your total balance.

Outstanding interest is the interest that has accrued since your last payment, whether you made a payment last month or 2 years ago because you're on an excused payment break.

Enrollment Status: Unless you went back to school, enrollment status won't affect you much now, but your child likely won't be able to consolidate their loans generally until they're out of school.

STEP 4: REVIEW YOUR LOAN CHART AND FIGURE OUT WHICH LOANS YOU STILL OWE MONEY ON

Your loan chart is on your personal home page after you successfully log on to the NSLDS. All your loans are listed in order from your newest to your oldest. Thus, if you've consolidated your loans into one or two new loans with one convenient payment, the consolidation loans will be listed first—unless you received more loans after you consolidated.

For example, if you went back to school for a graduate degree and went a little deeper into student loan debt, your graduate school loans would be newer than your consolidation loans. The reason you could see two consolidation loans instead of one is because consolidated loans are separated into subsidized and unsubsidized loans. This is in case you return to school or otherwise qualify for a temporary loan deferment—a reprieve from making payments in which the government pays your interest on the subsidized portion of your loan.

This doesn't mean that if you have all your loans consolidated with the same company that you won't make one payment. Your loan company divides the payment for you between the loans so you only have to think about making one payment. Now that you know how your loan chart is organized, scan through your loans and look for the loans in which you still have balances. Keep in mind that any of the loans you consolidated into one larger loan will show a $0 balance. At this point, you should print a copy of your own loan chart and highlight the loans that have balances in the Outstanding Principal column. You can figure out how much you owe on each loan by adding your outstanding principal with your outstanding interest owed.

Carefully scan your chart for loans that you may have missed in consolidation or forgotten about, and highlight those loans as well.

STEP 5: GATHER INFORMATION FROM YOUR INDIVIDUAL LOAN CHARTS

At this point, you know what you owe. Great start! Now, you need to dig deeper. When you click on individual loans in your chart, you'll find more charts. Exciting, right? Click on the number next to the loan you'd like information on to pull up charts on an individual loan.

Amounts and Dates Chart: The dates on the Amounts and Dates chart don't have to do with when you first took out your loan. Instead, the dates tell you what date the interest and principal amounts are based on. For example, if you just made a payment on February 10 and the interest and principal dates are January 31, you know that your interest and principal amounts are a little lower than reported on the chart. If you had part of your loan cancelled, the date of cancellation is also shown. While the Amounts and Dates chart doesn't show your actual interest rate, it does show whether your rate is fixed or variable. In 2006, all student loans started being issued with fixed rates, but any loans you have from before July 1, 2006, that aren't consolidated will have variable rates that are set annually on July 1.

Status Description: The status description box lets you see what's going on with your student debt, from the date your loan was issued to present day. You can also see on what dates the status changed, so if your loan went astray, you will know exactly when this happened. For instance, I had a default at one point because I missed a loan in consolidation. I didn't find out about the default for 10 years! If you have a loan that shows it's defaulted, you need to call the guaranty agency right away to discuss your options and get on a plan. If you're worried you can't make the payments required to get your loan out of default, there's good news: On July 1, 2014, a new income-based default rehabilitation started to help borrowers afford to repay defaulted loans.

Note: On your credit report, a defaulted loan is viewed similar to a charge-off, but it has much worse consequences because student loan debt generally cannot be expunged in bankruptcy. However, you can get your defaulted loan off your credit report with as few as 10 on-time payments.

Servicer/Lender/Guaranty Agency Chart: This chart contains all the contact information you need. The servicer is the company that handles customer service for the lender, even direct loans, and the company you are most in contact with. The guaranty company guarantees the loan for the lender. This is who you deal with once your loan has defaulted. You may also deal with a collection agency instead of a guaranty agency. But the information will be listed in the chart. For non-defaulted loans, you need the number for your servicer so you can call to ask questions about your interest rates, terms of your loan, your payment history, or the time left to finish paying off your loans.

Constructing Your Personal Student Loan Chart

By this point in the chapter, you may be experiencing chart overload. But I promise that this is the last one. I'm going to show you how to combine all your student loan information that you just read about into one chart. With your Personal Student Loan chart in front of you, you can evaluate repayment options and strategies for paying off your debt faster based on the debt you have. Get out a piece of paper to construct the chart manually or open up a spreadsheet in your favorite computer program. You can also create a table in your favorite word processing program. No matter which method you choose, you'll use the following format. In the rows, you'll list the loans for which you still owe balances. These are the ones you highlighted on your NSLDS loan chart after you printed it out. You'll assign each loan a number. Use the following as column titles:

Original Loan Date: In this column, put the date you first borrowed your loan.

Amount Owed: To find the amount you owe on an individual loan, add your outstanding principal with your outstanding interest.

Current Servicer: The name of the servicer listed for this loan in the Servicer/Lender/Guaranty Agency Information chart. (If you have a default, list the guaranty agency for this particular loan.)

Contact Information: The phone number listed for your servicer in the Servicer/Lender/Guaranty Agency Information chart.

Loan Type and Status: The information you need for this column is in your NSLDS loan chart under Type of Loan. The status is located in your Disbursement(s) and Status(es) chart under Status Description.

Interest Rate: To find out what interest rate you are currently paying on your loan, contact your servicer. While you're at it, ask if your rate is fixed or variable.

Monthly Payment: Before you hang up with your servicer, find out what your current monthly payment is.

If you constructed your chart on the computer, print out a copy and keep it in a folder along with exercises you'll complete in chapter 14. If you filled in the chart on a piece of paper, keep it in a notebook.

Disputing Information Contained on the National Student Loan Data System

This is another area where I can't emphasize enough what can happen when there's an error, but I also can't emphasize enough how easy it is to fix errors.

My default was a loan I didn't know about that wasn't consolidated. Years later, I don't remember if that one loan that wasn't included in my consolidation was my fault or someone else's. Now, all federal student loans are consolidated through direct lending. But back then, it could have been done by banks and lenders participating in the federal student loan system. This loan is now out of default and consolidated, and I'm making payments on it. A careful look at the NSLDS will help you fix these personal or lender/servicer or guaranty agency errors.

The three types of errors that can exist are double listings, inaccurate listings, and missing listings. If you have any of these errors or something appears off, call your loan servicer or guaranty agency if defaulted. If the problem isn't resolved or explained to you properly, call the federal student loan ombudsman. The ombudsman mediates disputes between you and the servicer or guaranty agency. The contact number is 1-877-557-2575. Always check the NSLDS every few months to make sure everything is being reported properly.

DOUBLE LISTINGS: A LOAN IS LISTED TWICE

If you've consolidated your loans, there might be one listing for the original loan, which you'll now see has a balance of $0. It could also be because your tuition was the same for both semesters of the same year, meaning the original amounts are identical because you borrowed the same amount two semesters in a row. However, like anything else, scrutinize this carefully, and make sure you read the columns. If you think something appears off, call the servicer of that loan and ask them to explain it you.

INACCURATE LISTINGS: A LOAN IS REPORTED INCORRECTLY

You may notice a loan on your report that you thought you'd paid off—and maybe you did. Check your old bank statements for when the payments could have been taken out. If you don't have your old bank statements, call your bank and order them. Just because you may have switched banks doesn't mean you can't find proof of your old payments. You can contact your former bank to gather old bank statements. Don't forget to check savings accounts or your parent's bank accounts that you may have made the payments out of as well.

Once you find the information you need, contact your servicer and your state's Department of Education to correct the problem. Calling the servicer is of the utmost importance; a mistake may have occurred in their computer system where they are still reporting that you owe them money when you don't. Luckily, if you have your bank statements handy when you call them, you'll have the proof you need ready to send them so they can correct the errors.

> ## Caution
>
> Don't ignore anything on your report that doesn't look right. You could stop making payments on a loan that you actually owe money on and go into default. Check with your state's Department of Education and your servicer to correct any errors, especially if you see a loan you thought you paid off that shows an amount owed. Then call your bank to order a record of past bill payments or cancelled checks for the payments if you are required to show proof of payments.

MISSING LISTINGS

If you don't see a loan on your report when you know you did borrow the money, this can feel like a big birthday present. But it doesn't mean you should not take action. Check your records and your bank statements to verify that you did borrow this money. Contact both your servicer and your state's Department of Education about the error if you find there is one.

Gathering Information on Your Child's Federal Student Loans

Direct your child to follow the same steps you did to create their own Personal Student Loan chart. I talk about creating a separate chart for private student loans in the next chapter. When looking up monthly payments on your child's loans if they've yet to graduate, your child should calculate potential payments with the repayment estimator (log on to studentloans.gov). If you're considering helping them by paying part or all of their payments, you will definitely want to see this chart as well as the one they'll create for private loans. Remember, you can switch repayment plans at any time. So can your children.

Loan Payment Options and Public Service Loan Forgiveness

Unfortunately, not all payment plan options that are available to students are also available to parents. So before you decide to combine your parent PLUS loans with your other student loans, take a look at repayment plan options as well what your payment would be under consolidation.

REPAYMENT PLAN OPTIONS

The Standard 10-Year Plan

Your loans are automatically put on a 10-year repayment plan if you don't select an alternate repayment plan option. However, if you have a large amount of debt, this plan can be quite pricey for your budget. For instance, if you borrowed $80,000 at a 6.8 percent interest rate, your payments would be over $900 per month.

Income-Related Plans

Income-related repayment plans base payments on the amount of debt you can handle in relation to your income. There are a variety of income-related plans for which you may be eligible. The income-contingent repayment plan is based on a larger percentage of discretionary income. You don't need to know how the government determines discretionary income. Use the online repayment estimator discussed later in this chapter

Caution

Changes are coming in December 2015 to the Pay as You Earn program that may help you qualify on loans that you borrowed for your own education. Whenever, a new program starts, call your servicer to see if your loans qualify.

to estimate payments. Once your loans are borrowed, the calculator offers you a chance to log in and get information based on your actual loans.

Since loans you borrowed for your own education may qualify for a better income-related plan, you might want to consolidate loans that were for your education separately.

CONSOLIDATION

Consolidation generally means combining two or more loans into one loan with one payment. Once consolidated, you can choose among a variety of payment time frames. And you can always pay off the loan early without penalty. If you only have parent PLUS loans, you can only qualify for an extended or consolidated plan. You can't qualify for most income-related options. This may not be much of a concern if you borrowed a reasonable amount of debt and don't qualify for Public Service Loan Forgiveness. Plus, you have options to extend payments up to 30 years, depending on the amount you borrowed. To extend payments this long, you'll have to pick one of the consolidated options.

PUBLIC SERVICE LOAN FORGIVENESS

Public Service Loan Forgiveness is a nifty program for those who work for the government, a nonprofit business [501(c3)], or a specific career field such as healthcare. The program allows you to make 10 years of student loan payments with either an income-related or standard repayment plan. After 10 years, the rest of the loan balance is forgiven. You need to have direct loans to qualify. You can consolidate your loans to direct lending to qualify, even if it's just one.

If you have any inkling that you might qualify for Public Service Loan Forgiveness and you have your own student loans, too, you'll want to choose an income-related plan such as income-contingent repayments. Pay as You Earn or income-based plans don't work with parent PLUS loans currently. If you choose a standard 10-year repayment, you probably won't see much benefit from getting the remainder of your loans forgiven after 10 years of on-time payments.

Many people think they don't qualify for Public Service Loan Forgiveness, but a quarter of borrowers do. Why all the confusion? Often, people think they need to be employed by a nonprofit business or a government agency in a public service field such as healthcare to qualify. However, the marketing person at a private hospital qualifies. If you think you might qualify for Public Service Loan Forgiveness you should fill out the employment certification form application just in case. You can find links to the application on the resources page of graduationdebt.org.

Here are some important facts about Public Service Loan Forgiveness that you should know:

- Parent PLUS loans qualify for the income-contingent income-related program, whether or not the loan is consolidated with the parent's own student loans. Remember, a consolidated loan is eligible, but any kind of extended plan not related to income is not.

- It's not true that you'll start the clock over if you take a break from public service employment. The clock is just paused. However, if you consolidate your loan that would have qualified into a new loan, you will start the clock over. If consolidated with parent PLUS loans, you may raise your payment in addition to starting the clock over if you previously qualified for a cheaper income-related plan.

- You may have already made some qualifying payments: Payments made on October 2, 2007, or later count toward the 120 payments required to earn Public Service Loan Forgiveness.

- It's all or nothing. You can't be partially forgiven under the Public Service Loan Forgiveness program.

Other public service forgiveness programs may be offered on the state level. Contact your state's Department of Education about other programs offered. Also, check with your employer's human resources department about programs for tuition reimbursement and scholarships for your child.

Note: As of December 2015, you may be eligible for the Pay as You Earn program, which is cheaper than the income-based repayment plan. Before the eligibility change, you would have to have gone to school recently to qualify for the lower income-related payments. It also has a maximum payoff time of 20 years as opposed to 25 years.

Calculating Payments

There are two websites to calculate payment options if you choose a different repayment plan than the one you are on: studentloans.gov's repayment estimator (www.studentaid.ed.gov/repay-loans) and the consolidation calculator at loanconsolidation.ed.gov.

USING THE REPAYMENT ESTIMATOR

The repayment estimator allows you to compare income-related options with basic extended and 10-year repayment options. For instance, if you are single with an adjusted gross income of $80,000 and owe $80,000 with a 7 percent interest rate, you'd possibly qualify for a payment ranging from $521 per month on Pay as You Earn if it's for your loans for your education to a 25-year payment of $568 per month. To double-check the amounts owed, you'll want to verify with your servicer.

The problem with income-related options such as Pay as You Earn is that they can rise as your income rises, all the way up to a payment—in this case, that's over $1,000. You can also owe interest from the time period you were on an income-related plan if your payment wasn't enough to cover it. However, they are generally worth it if you have any chance of qualifying for Public Service Loan Forgiveness.

You can also go to the consolidation calculator and see what your payment would be. No matter what your income is, your payment would be $532.

Early Payoff Strategies

There are several ways to pay off student loans early with relatively little impact on your lifestyle. Here are four of the best ways to pay off loans early.

REBATE AND REWARDS PROGRAMS

Many credit cards offer cash-back programs. Why not dedicate part of your cash back toward student loan repayment? At the same time join Upromise and get rebates on the purchases you'd make anyway online, on real estate, and in restaurants and grocery stores. I know people who've accumulated $300 or more this way without adding extra purchases.

> **Caution**
>
> Always balance paying off student loans faster with other priorities in your life. Your retirement shouldn't suffer, and you should pay off high-interest credit card debt first.

TAX REFUNDS

You can easily get back $2,500 per year from the American Opportunity Tax Credit for the years that your child was in school. And you can amend returns for up to 3 years if you forgot to claim the credit.

But there's more tax fun. You can get back up to another $625 or so from the student loan tax deduction. You can claim loans you took out for yourself as well as parent PLUS or private loans you took out for your child that are in your name while they were still a dependent.

For instance, if you borrowed a parent PLUS loan in a year that you claimed your college-age student as a dependent on your tax return, you can deduct interest you pay in future years as well. However, if you didn't claim your child as a dependent, you can never claim interest you paid on your child's loan for the purpose of the deduction. If you cosigned a loan, you can't claim the deduction because, according to the IRS, the loan belongs to the student.

Review the current year's income guidelines for being able to deduct student loan interest on www.irs.gov. Just do a quick search for Publication 970.

> ### Caution
>
> You can amend tax returns for up to 3 years, so don't assume you're out the money if you missed a credit or a deduction or neglected to claim your child as a dependent. However, you may want to consult an accountant before amending returns.

REMAINING 529 PLAN ACCOUNT BALANCES

If your child is done with college, why not cash out remaining dollars to pay off student loans? The only problem is there is a 10 percent tax penalty on the balance, and then you have to pay income tax on the earnings. But, hey—it's better than the money just sitting there if you don't have a use for it for another family member's education.

Example of the tax penalty: The account has a $10,000 balance. You're charged an instant penalty of $1,000. But then $5,000 of the $10,000 was from account earnings, money earned off of the original balance. Your tax bracket is 25 percent. You're charged an additional 25 percent of $5,000: $1,250. $10,000 – $1,000 – $1,250 = $7,750. That's a nice chunk of money to use toward student loan repayment. However, you should talk to your children about whether the money will be used for their loans or yours.

A Few Dollars at a Time

Start small by adding $5, $10, or $20 to your monthly payment. How could as little as $5 extra a month help you pay off your student loans faster? The amount you owe will be reduced by each $5 you add to your payments, but you'll also reduce your total bill by the interest you would be charged on that amount of money. For example, at a 6 percent interest rate for 30 years, $5 of your loan would cost almost $24 to borrow. That's three times your payment! Think about how much you'd save by paying $5 extra every month. Now, not every $5 will save you $24 in interest. This is because if you have a higher interest rate, you are charged more in interest to borrow that $5. If you have a lower interest rate, you are charged less. Remember, you don't want to add extra dollars if you expect some degree of Public Service Loan Forgiveness.

Check out the following table to see how making additional small monthly payments in year five of these consolidated loans would make a difference in how fast the loans are paid off.

	Time Saved Off Loan by Adding $5 per Month	Time Saved Off Loan by Adding $10 per Month	Time Saved Off Loan by Adding $20 per Month
$50,000 consolidated at 4% (25-year loan)	9 months	18 months	34 months
$60,000 consolidated at 4% (30-year loan)	11 months	22 months	42 months
$70,000 consolidated at 5% (30-year loan)	10 months	20 months	38 months
$80,000 consolidated at 5% (30-year loan)	9 months	18 months	34 months

Chapter Wrap-Up

$ The National Student Loan Data System (NSLDS) is the place to go to find your federal student loan information, including contact information for your servicers to ask questions such as what your interest rate is.

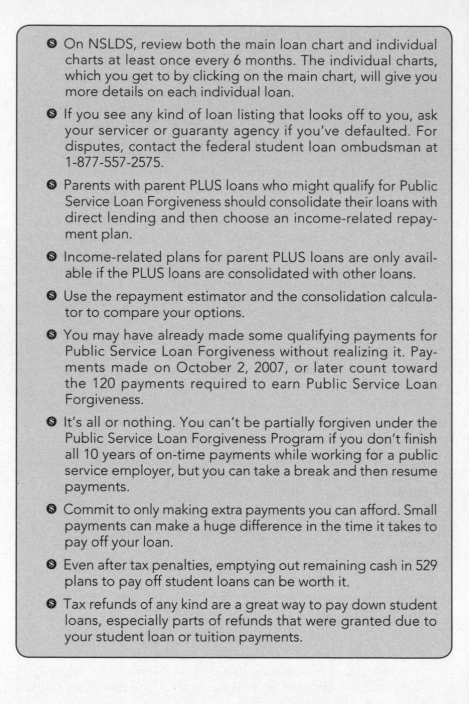

- On NSLDS, review both the main loan chart and individual charts at least once every 6 months. The individual charts, which you get to by clicking on the main chart, will give you more details on each individual loan.

- If you see any kind of loan listing that looks off to you, ask your servicer or guaranty agency if you've defaulted. For disputes, contact the federal student loan ombudsman at 1-877-557-2575.

- Parents with parent PLUS loans who might qualify for Public Service Loan Forgiveness should consolidate their loans with direct lending and then choose an income-related repayment plan.

- Income-related plans for parent PLUS loans are only available if the PLUS loans are consolidated with other loans.

- Use the repayment estimator and the consolidation calculator to compare your options.

- You may have already made some qualifying payments for Public Service Loan Forgiveness without realizing it. Payments made on October 2, 2007, or later count toward the 120 payments required to earn Public Service Loan Forgiveness.

- It's all or nothing. You can't be partially forgiven under the Public Service Loan Forgiveness Program if you don't finish all 10 years of on-time payments while working for a public service employer, but you can take a break and then resume payments.

- Commit to only making extra payments you can afford. Small payments can make a huge difference in the time it takes to pay off your loan.

- Even after tax penalties, emptying out remaining cash in 529 plans to pay off student loans can be worth it.

- Tax refunds of any kind are a great way to pay down student loans, especially parts of refunds that were granted due to your student loan or tuition payments.

Repaying Private Student Loans

If you borrowed for your own education, the idea of paying off your education debt plus your child's may seem overwhelming. The good news is you don't have to pay off your child's loans for them, but you do need to help them plan repayment. You also need to be prepared to pay for their loans if they can't for at least the first 1 to 2 years. Why?

The altruistic reason is because you want your child to do well in life, and helping them figure out their loan payments now will help keep them from still living in your basement at age 40.

The second reason is you more than likely cosigned for your child, meaning until you're released from responsability for paying off these loans, you and your credit report are going to reap the repercussions if payments aren't made.

In this chapter, I tell you the basics of private student loan repayment that are important for both you and your child, help you develop a plan for repayment, and explain how to get released as a cosigner. Finally, I cover creating an overall repayment plan for both federal and private student loans.

Private Student Loan Basics

Whether you've been making payments on your private student loans for 10 years or are about to make your first payment, there are things you need to know about your loan. There are three places to find out the information you need: your credit reports, your contract, and your loan servicer. These are the same places your child will need to look in order to find out about their student loans.

Remember, until a cosigner agreement expires, you should also know all this information for loans you cosigned for your child.

YOUR CREDIT REPORTS

You can pull up your credit reports for free on www.annualcreditreport. com. You will be asked for basic information to verify your identity, such as former addresses or what cars you've owned. It's always good to try to recall the information before pulling up the website so your session doesn't time out while you're scrambling to find the information to enter.

When you view each of the three reports from the major credit bureaus (Experian, TransUnion, and Equifax), make sure your loan payments are reported correctly. For instance, does it show a late payment or no payment at all when you thought you'd made payments? You need to check bank statements and call your servicer right away if there's a discrepancy. Ask your servicer to send a correction to the credit bureaus. Then reorder credit reports a few months later to make sure everything's fixed.

You should also make sure that there isn't a stray loan you forgot about and that your federal student loans are being reported as well. Remember to also help your child with this process.

Note: You may see a late payment on a loan you cosigned for your child. Before calling the servicer, talk to your child about whether or not they're making their payments. I talk more about cosigning and repayment later in this chapter.

YOUR LOAN CONTRACT

Now, pull out the contract you signed. Look for the repayment terms. You'll need to find out the following:

How long is your current repayment period? For instance, is it 5, 10, or 15 years?

How long was the repayment term originally? The reason why it would have changed is if you were granted a payment break such as a reduced payment for a specified period of time or an extension in order to reduce the amount of your monthly payment.

How did late fees and interest rate hikes alter the length of repayment in the past? This is relevant if your loan term changes affected your repayment terms in any way.

How long could a late payment or interest rate hike alter repayment time frames or amounts in the future? This is especially important for you to go over with your child concerning their loans so they know how high the payment could go. Refer to pages 95–98 in chapter 10 for information on how much interest rates could rise and how it would affect your payments. It doesn't mean interest rates *will* rise, but they could, and you may only get a month or two's notice.

IMPORTANT NOTE: In the last few years, the Consumer Financial Protection Bureau has started helping private student loan borrowers resolve disputes with their loan servicers. If your private student loan servicer doesn't fix an error on your credit report, contact the Bureau online at help.consumerfinance.gov/app/studentloan/ask. You'll need bank statements or other proof that there was an error, and they'll help you resolve it.

YOUR SERVICER

If you can't locate your loan contract or if you have questions, you should contact the servicer. Have your lender fax or mail you the contract if you no longer have it, so you know exactly what your terms of loan repayment are.

Don't rely on what is said over the phone. For anything a customer service associate tells you, make sure you can also locate this information in your contract. Most likely, you will be given accurate information regarding the term length and late-fee rules, but you don't want to risk it. A customer service associate could accidentally misstate something.

By having the terms in writing, you don't have to worry about forgetting or confusing what was said to you over the phone when you're overloaded with the loan terms of three or more different banks.

You also want to ask your servicer if you can get an interest rate adjustment if you make a specified number of on-time payments.

IMPORTANT NOTE: Private loans are now available to parents, too. For instance, private student loan company SoFi, piloted in 2014 at Standford University, is now available to families with students attending one of over 2,200 schools. Check out these loans as an alternative to PLUS. The one drawback? You won't have any options for income-related repayment plans or financial hardship.

Financial Hardship

If you're having trouble paying your federal loans and you call your servicer to discuss your options, the process is fairly easy. You will most likely be asked a few questions and then be offered forbearance or deferment (the two types of payment breaks) for a few months or even a year. You may still owe the interest, but you get a break from making payments to catch up on your other bills, possibly pay down your high-interest credit card debt, or find a new job if you lost your old one.

However, if you made the same call to a private student loan lender, you would probably not have the same ease in postponing payments. And if your child wants a temporary break from their private loan payments, your income will likely be considered if you're still a cosigner. After you're removed from the loan through a cosigner release program (see page 151 for more information), temporary payment breaks are based solely on your child's financial circumstances.

The good news is that many private loan servicers do work with borrowers on repayment, especially during tough times, when the sheer number of borrowers experiencing financial hardship demands it. It's likely that you or your child could get private loan forbearance, if the private loan servicer you chose offers it, for a few months or even a year—especially if it's due to your income being reduced as opposed to your child's income. A temporary reduced payment schedule based on your financial circumstances may be available as well.

If you have a mix of private and federal student loans, also consider getting forbearance on your federal loans when you are in a financial bind. Let your child know to do the same on their loans. This will allow you or your child, depending on whose loans they are, to make payments on your private loans that may have less flexibility than your federal loans do for financial hardship situations.

The bottom line is that you won't know what your options are unless you read your paperwork and ask questions. In other words, think of a financial hardship situation as if you were taking a tough college course. If you're having trouble and you never ask your professor about the material you don't understand, you'll end up failing the course. However, if you ask a few questions during class you may come out with a good grade. Dealing with a financial hardship situation when you have a private student loan works in the same way. Research and ask questions, and you'll get through it.

Keep in mind that if you didn't make your payments for a period of time during the course of your repayment term, interest still accrues without a payment being made to counteract it. Late fees may also be charged. Thus, your repayment period may also be extended. If you are in a situation where you are behind on your payments, ask your private loan lender how long it would take to repay the loan if your payments stayed on course.

Options for Paying Off or Transferring Private Loan Debt

It's tempting to want to consolidate private student loans or pay them off with a 0 percent credit card offer. Sometimes one or both is a good idea, but these options should be considered carefully.

> ### Caution
>
> When cosigning a consolidation loan for your child, make sure there is a cosigner release form on the new loan.

CREDIT CARD TRANSFERS

If you have great credit, take advantage of it. Have you seen any credit card offers for 0 percent for 12 months or 4.9 to 6.9 percent for the life of your loan in your mailbox lately? Transfer as much as you can to one of these cards to save on interest accrued. However, there are some cautions that you should heed:

- **Don't transfer more to a 12-month offer than you can reasonably pay off in a year because your interest rate will increase on the remaining balance of what you transferred to your credit card when the 12-month period is over.** For example, if you have $300 left over at the end of each month after putting away money for savings, you can transfer $3,600 to a credit card on a 12-month offer at 0 percent.

- **Budget so that you can make payments on the private loan balance you weren't able to transfer at the same time as your credit card payment.** You don't want your plan to save you money in interest but cost you a bundle in late fees for delayed payments while you shuffle your debt to make your regular payments on your loan. Remember, no matter how much of your private loan you transfer, your payment may not drop proportionately. This is because while the principal on your loan drops, your variable interest rate on your private loan could rise the next month.

- **When budgeting to see how much you could afford to pay off through a balance transfer, don't use your current month's payment.** If your interest rate on your private loans rises, you could throw your entire budget out of whack. Remember how your interest rate terms work and calculate what your payment would be if your interest rate jumped 5 percent for a LIBOR-based loan or 6 percent for a prime-based loan. (Refer to chapter 10 for how your interest terms work.)

- **Know what your balance transfer fees are.** You won't do yourself any good unless you know exactly what you are paying. For instance, let's say your 0 percent interest offer comes with a balance transfer fee of 4 percent. If you transfer $5,000, you're charged $200 right off the bat to borrow the money. This is equivalent to the interest you would pay in 1 year to pay off $5,000 at 7.31 percent interest. Unless your terms currently have an interest rate that is higher than this, you shouldn't be doing a balance transfer.

  Always compare the interest that would be charged to the balance transfer fee. Using a simple loan calculator on your bank's website, enter your current interest rate with the amount you want to borrow and 12 months. If this number is lower than your balance transfer fee, you may not want to do the balance transfer at this time. If it's within $20 or $30, you may want to do it just to secure a fixed interest rate on part of your loan.

- **If you plan on buying a new home or vehicle in the near future, only transfer enough that you won't go over 15 percent of your credit limit on your card.** This is because your credit score is partially determined by the percentage of your available credit that is used. Getting a lower interest rate on part of your loan won't help you if it affects whether you qualify for a home loan.

Consolidating Private Student Loans

Just like federal loans, your private loans can be consolidated. Similar to federal loans, consolidation will streamline your payments into one payment for all your private loans and reduce the amount you pay each month because your repayment period will be stretched out over a longer term. One way your private loans differ is that your new interest rate terms or fixed interest rate may not have anything to do with your previous fixed interest rate or interest rate terms. This is because federal loan consolidation rates are merely the average rate of the federal loans you are consolidating.

Note: Since all federal consolidation loans have fixed interest rates, I refer to these loans as having interest rates instead of interest rate terms. Private loans may have fixed interest rates or interest rate terms. In chapter 10, I talk about how to calculate what your payment range could be.

When consolidating a private loan, you'll get new interest rate terms based on what is currently being offered, and your credit and payment history will likely be reconsidered. The bright side is that you can get quotes from different loan companies, just as you would if you were refinancing a mortgage. Also, if your credit has improved since you originally borrowed your loan, you could get better terms or no longer need to have a cosigner. For example, let's say you currently have $60,000 in private loans with terms of 1-month LIBOR plus 10 percent. Your credit has improved, and you can now get terms of 1-month LIBOR plus 4 percent. The 6 percent difference in your margin could save you up to $300 a month on your extended 30-year loan versus an extended plan at your old terms. The money you'd save is regardless of how much your interest rate might vary.

How do you find the right bank and the best deal when refinancing your loan? Here are some tips:

- **Don't limit yourself to your current lenders.** With a private loan, you can call up any bank that offers private consolidation loans to get a quote. Start by calling your current lenders, then your current bank, and then do an online search for private consolidation loans. Get at least three different quotes.

- **If you are considering consolidating, make a photocopy of your Personal Student Loan Chart that you created in chapter 13.** Then on the photocopy, add rows to the chart. Add a column

> ### Caution
>
> Don't give personal information to any bank you haven't heard of that offers you a consolidation loan until you've double-checked its legitimacy, either through your state's commission that regulates lending or the Better Business Bureau. Also, beware of companies offering to consolidate your federal student loans. It may sound like a good deal, but make sure the interest rate or interest terms make up for the federal student loan perks of programs for special repayment plans and payment breaks when you hit financial snags.

for origination fees, too. This way you can compare them on one sheet of paper.

- **Pay attention to both the margin and the index.** For instance, you don't want to sign up for a prime rate loan with the same margin added to it as a LIBOR-based loan. Historically the difference between the two could be 2.5 to 3 percent.

Here are some questions you should be sure to ask lenders before consolidating:

- **Is there a loan origination fee?** A loan origination fee means the lender will charge you a percentage of your loan when you take out your new consolidation. For example, if you owe $60,000 and the loan origination fee is 1 percent, you will be charged $600 for the consolidation. Sometimes a loan origination fee can be worth it. For example, let's say in your consolidated loan, the margin portion of your interest rate terms is 1 percent lower. You would pay $600 to consolidate your loans, but would save $600 this year and 1 percent of the balance each following year.

- **Will you consolidate loans from other banks?** If you have loans from more than one lender, ask each new lender you are considering if they will also take on your other private loans.

- **How long is the new repayment period?** You need to know just how long it will take you to repay the loan with your extended repayment period.

- **What circumstances will cause a change in the interest rate, such as a late or missed payment?** How much would your interest rate increase in this situation?

REFOCUSING YOUR BUDGET TO PAY OFF YOUR LOANS

You should follow the same rules for making budget changes as I've discussed in previous chapters, especially focusing on your overall financial picture. Then spend part of what you have left over on repaying private student loans first when it comes to paying off loans early. Remember, this is about your loans, not your child's loans. However, they should also do this for their own loans.

For instance, if you have a few dollars left at the end of the month that aren't otherwise allocated, put that cash toward your private student loan debt if it has a variable interest rate instead of fixed rate car loans or federal student loans. The less money you are loaned at a variable rate, the better. Even adding $5 or $10 will help toward paying off your loan, but don't refocus your budget so much that you end up paying late fees on other loans or having no cushion in your savings or checking account. My favorite way to pay off loans faster is by using tax refund money that was a result of education tuition or student loan interest deductions.

Getting Released as a Cosigner from Your Student's Private Student Loans

When it comes to budgeting for your child's private loans, you should budget for them until the date the cosigner agreement ends for on-time payments. The time frame for cosigner release generally ranges anywhere from 12 to 24 months. You don't necessarily have to pay their loans during those early months, but you do have to budget for them.

For example, if the loan you cosigned for your child has a fixed interest rate with a monthly payment of $300, you should budget for that payment until you're released as cosigner. You may well end up with $7,200 of savings because your child made every single payment without your help.

Your child will also need to have good credit, so emphasize that they shouldn't let their credit card balances get above 15 percent of the limit.

Now, the hard part for many parents: the monthly talk about whether your child is making their loan payments on time. It may seem like you don't trust your child, but you need to have a monthly discussion with your child about whether they are able to make their payments. Make it as casual as possible and tell them they can simply text you on a monthly basis to let you know the payment was made. Also, let them know that you will help as needed for the length of the cosigner agreement without judgment. However, the condition for help needs to be that you can talk to them about their budget on a monthly basis. Other options include requiring that they take a free online budgeting course, visit with a credit union financial counselor to develop a budget, or talk to their school's student money management office.

Create a Chart of All of Your Loan Payments and Information

Remember the Personal Student Loan chart that you created in chapter 13? Now, you just need to add a few more columns for pertinent information about private loans, including the following:

- **Cosigner release time frame.** If this is your own loan versus your student's, you can leave this blank.

- **Payment for your student's private loans.** You need to know the payment amount just in case you have to make the payment for the first 1 or 2 years.

- **Amount you'd like to budget for repaying loans faster.** You can decide later how you want to distribute this amount.

- **Interest rate terms.** You need to know when and how your loan's interest rate can change (see chapter 10, pages 95–98).

- **Availability of extended payment option.** Call your loan servicer and ask what extended payment plans are available. For instance, could you switch to a 15- or 30-year plan later if you needed to?

- **Amount the student will contribute.** This is needed if you have a long-term agreement with your child for them to help with loans under your name. If you help them create their charts, they'd have a similar category for how much you'd contribute.

Caution

If you're helping your student figure out their budget for private student loans, remind them that if their rate is variable, it can change at time periods set by the lender or servicer. These time frames are generally 30 to 90 days. If you're setting up direct debit payments, it's very important that the student understands and is prepared for any jumps. The good news is that rates and payments can also decline, but it's important to be prepared for any potential scenarios.

Chapter Wrap-Up

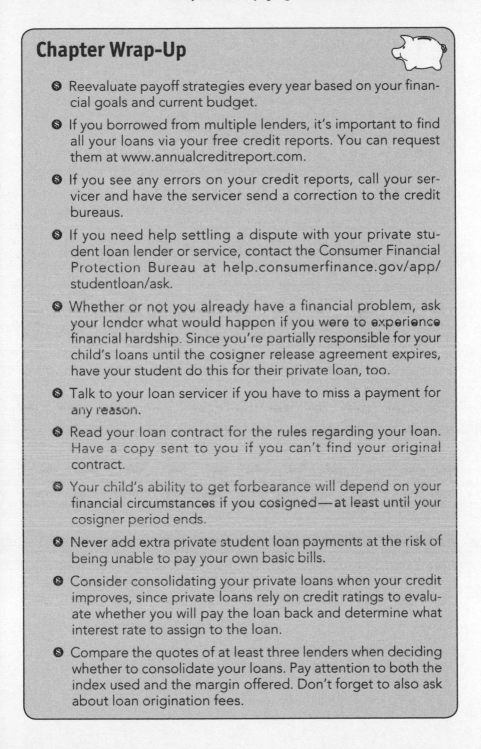

- Reevaluate payoff strategies every year based on your financial goals and current budget.

- If you borrowed from multiple lenders, it's important to find all your loans via your free credit reports. You can request them at www.annualcreditreport.com.

- If you see any errors on your credit reports, call your servicer and have the servicer send a correction to the credit bureaus.

- If you need help settling a dispute with your private student loan lender or service, contact the Consumer Financial Protection Bureau at help.consumerfinance.gov/app/studentloan/ask.

- Whether or not you already have a financial problem, ask your lender what would happen if you were to experience financial hardship. Since you're partially responsible for your child's loans until the cosigner release agreement expires, have your student do this for their private loan, too.

- Talk to your loan servicer if you have to miss a payment for any reason.

- Read your loan contract for the rules regarding your loan. Have a copy sent to you if you can't find your original contract.

- Your child's ability to get forbearance will depend on your financial circumstances if you cosigned—at least until your cosigner period ends.

- Never add extra private student loan payments at the risk of being unable to pay your own basic bills.

- Consider consolidating your private loans when your credit improves, since private loans rely on credit ratings to evaluate whether you will pay the loan back and determine what interest rate to assign to the loan.

- Compare the quotes of at least three lenders when deciding whether to consolidate your loans. Pay attention to both the index used and the margin offered. Don't forget to also ask about loan origination fees.

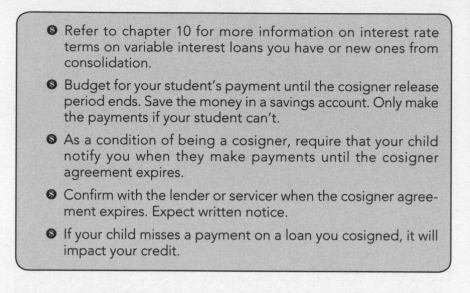

- Refer to chapter 10 for more information on interest rate terms on variable interest loans you have or new ones from consolidation.

- Budget for your student's payment until the cosigner release period ends. Save the money in a savings account. Only make the payments if your student can't.

- As a condition of being a cosigner, require that your child notify you when they make payments until the cosigner agreement expires.

- Confirm with the lender or servicer when the cosigner agreement expires. Expect written notice.

- If your child misses a payment on a loan you cosigned, it will impact your credit.

Looking to the Future: Saving or Planning for Continuing Education

As much as we'd like to think we're done with all education and training after graduating college, whether we complete an associate's degree or even a Ph.D., that's often not the case. Pretty much all professionals will require some additional training at some point to keep up with technology and other changes in their field.

So as a parent, should you save for your child's education? And what about your own?

In this chapter I talk about when and how to save for continuing education for yourself and your child. I also cover some free options for continuing education.

Reducing Continuing Education Costs Through Workplace Programs

You should always seek out new opportunities to learn. Many employers provide training to their employees. Check with human resources and ask what programs are available for continuing your education via additional college courses and general workplace development. Your employer may pay for you to go to seminars or even pay the tuition for a full master's degree. The same advice works for your child post-college. Also, there may be on-site opportunities for career development or online programs to further develop skills, ranging from computer skills to team building.

There's also on-the-job learning. People often feel the need to return to school because they feel stuck in a career rut. Asking for extra responsibilities or applying for a different job within the same company tackles three problems: boredom, financing, and developing additional skills that can lead to more advancement opportunities.

Within the on-the-job training realm is learning from your coworkers. For instance, I've learned so much at conferences; I sign up to be a mentor and get a mentor. My first book, *CliffsNotes Graduation Debt: How to Manage Student Loans and Live Your Life*, was a result of a mentoring meeting at a conference 8 years ago. My mentor told me I needed to write it and taught me how to get an agent. I owe half of my career to a 30-minute meeting with Peggy.

On the other hand, I've learned so much from those I've mentored. They give me great input on what financial issues current college students have. Technology equipment wasn't the expense back then that it is now.

Bottom line: Start with free ways to get additional education, beginning with workplace education opportunities, before getting into more debt or depleting part of your savings.

Estimating Continuing Education Costs

There are different forms of education you or your child will need when moving along a career path. One of the most common is continuing education. The range of continuing education requirements may vary, depending on your career field and whether or not you change professions.

THE PROFESSIONAL ORGANIZATIONS IN YOUR FIELD

Professional organizations often offer, or know who does offer, the continuing education you need to maintain licenses or retain organization memberships. By this point in your career, you probably know what continuing education is required. However, your recent grad should contact their professional organization.

The next step is to contact the places that teach the professional education and get a price estimate. Then add up totals for annual costs.

Some professions such as teaching often offer raises for a master's-level education. If this is the case, your recent grad or you—if you're the one needing the extra degree for a career boost—should compare the cost of the extra education to the extra income earned. For example, if the annual raise will be $5,000, and the degree costs $20,000 in tuition, fees, and textbooks, you'll have the money back in 4 years—totally worth it. If you're able to qualify for the Lifetime Learning Credit, you may get $4,000 back on your taxes from a 2-year program. To learn more about the Lifetime Learning Credit, go to www.irs.gov and search for Publication 970.

Some Course Options

COMMUNITY COLLEGE PROGRAMS

Community colleges are offering more programs than ever for professional development. Some colleges even have special course offerings that can help those with master's degrees fill in skill gaps.

For instance, someone who graduated college more than 10 years ago probably wasn't trained to work in teams. Rio Salado College, an online community college, offers reasonable tuition to develop business skills. Individuals who already have master's degrees often take the courses as much as anyone else. While the college is in Arizona, tuition is low enough for it to be accessible to out-of-state residents.

Community colleges are designing whole programs for employers to educate their employees on skill gaps for their industry. Check with your local community college for courses you can take, but also talk to your human resources department to see what training programs may be coming up.

FREE ONLINE COURSES

Have you always wanted to take a course at Harvard or Stanford? Well, there are now online courses offered free from these elite institutions. Harvard offers a free computer course, while Stanford offers free business courses.

The catch? You're not going to get the personal attention you would if you attended in person, but why not see what you can glean from watching these professors online?

GRADUATE CERTIFICATES

You can earn a graduate certificate in as little as 12 credits that may provide the training needed for you to change careers or advance within your career field. Pursuing a graduate certificate is also a great way to see if you really want to pursue the full 36-credit master's degree.

Weighing 529 Plan Use and Penalties

As a parent, you need to consider your own graduate school and career ambitions when deciding how much to pay for your child. For example, after your child has earned their undergraduate degree, you may decide to change your 529 plan beneficiary so you can use some money for yourself, your spouse, or for another child.

However, not all courses can be taken with 529 plan funds. For instance, a continuing education course may not qualify. However, courses that earn you college credits at an accredited college or university would. (To find out if the courses you or your child is considering would be eligible for credit at an accredited institution, go to https://fafsa.ed.gov/FAFSA/app/schoolSearch.) Figuring out what side of things your continuing education needs fall on for your profession will be helpful in determining how best to use leftover 529 plan funds.

Remember that there is a tax penalty if you withdraw money for something that is not a qualified education expense. Thus, if no one uses the leftover 529 plan money, you'll pay 10 percent of the amount you're withdrawing, plus income tax on the earnings on the account. Basically, you're paying capital gains on the growth of the account on earnings that would have been tax-exempt if used for education.

Don't let the tax penalty deter you from ever withdrawing anything from the account. It just means you should wait until you know without a doubt that you won't have an educational purpose for the money. There's no sense in paying a tax penalty if you can avoid it, but also no sense in never withdrawing the money because you don't want to pay the taxes.

Continuing Education Because of a Complete Change of Career

To decide if you'll need leftover 529 plan funds to continue your own education, start with a career evaluation. Are you happy with what you're doing now? Have you ruled out all jobs within your company? Here are some more questions you should ask yourself to help you decide:

Could you switch jobs without another degree? You might be able to apply your existing skills to a different career. It's not uncommon to perform a job that isn't typical of the degree you hold. For example, how many philosophy majors end up being professional philosophers?

A great way to explore this is to talk to friends whose careers you've always admired. Also talk to a career coach about how you could utilize your skills elsewhere. Your alumni career center is a great place to start. They'll still help you find work 50 years after graduation, or at least tell you what retraining you may need.

When I was doing party planning years ago, I was told all I really needed was a $1,000 course held outside of the university to gain my certification. That was a much better price than $10,000 for a hospitality master's that wouldn't have helped me fulfill my goal. There are also independent career coaches. Look up reviews online first and start with purchasing one appointment or participate in a free phone call before purchasing multiple hours of coaching.

Do you have a clear focus on what you want to do? Neither you nor your child should go back for another degree without a clear focus on what you want to do with the degree when you finish and a firm handle on the job outlook. If you are getting another degree to figure out what you want to do next, you might just get deeper into a student loan money pit. Which brings me to the next question...

Have you done a thorough review of incomes for the jobs you expect to garner with the degree you want? Before moving forward, you'll need to determine if you will make enough in this field right out of school to pay off current and future loans. You can find out the answer with research from the school career office or on salary.com or by talking to people in the field.

What about volunteer work in your spare time? Charities always need help, and volunteering is a great way to develop entirely new skill sets.

Have you talked to your alumni association? They can connect you with someone in the career field you're considering and advise on the education you'd need to pursue it.

If you or your child decide to back to school, utilize some of the same options you used when you first went to school: Look for scholarships and co-op programs. Choose colleges based on tuition as well as program quality. Going back to school can work out for you financially in the long run. Just do everything you can to make sure returning to school is the best decision for you before making another leap into more debt.

Chapter Wrap-Up

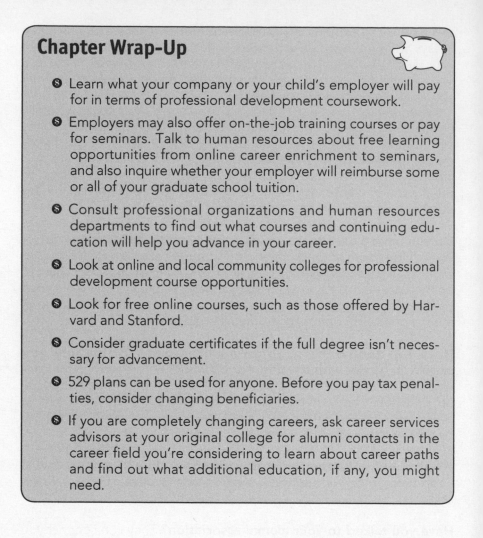

- Learn what your company or your child's employer will pay for in terms of professional development coursework.

- Employers may also offer on-the-job training courses or pay for seminars. Talk to human resources about free learning opportunities from online career enrichment to seminars, and also inquire whether your employer will reimburse some or all of your graduate school tuition.

- Consult professional organizations and human resources departments to find out what courses and continuing education will help you advance in your career.

- Look at online and local community colleges for professional development course opportunities.

- Look for free online courses, such as those offered by Harvard and Stanford.

- Consider graduate certificates if the full degree isn't necessary for advancement.

- 529 plans can be used for anyone. Before you pay tax penalties, consider changing beneficiaries.

- If you are completely changing careers, ask career services advisors at your original college for alumni contacts in the career field you're considering to learn about career paths and find out what additional education, if any, you might need.

Index